THE SUSAN AWARDS

A SELECTION OF WINNING WRITING

Book Design & Production:
Columbus Publishing Lab
www.ColumbusPublishingLab.com

Copyright © 2024 by
Jim Mahoney

Paperback ISBN: 978-1-63337-934-3
E-Book ISBN:978-1-63337-840-7

Printed in the United States of America
1 3 5 7 9 10 8 6 4 2

Cover artwork by Maggie Meyer, an eighth grader at the
time of this publication, and Susan Mahoney's niece.
Special thanks to her for lending her talents.

THE SUSAN AWARDS

A SELECTION OF WINNING WRITING

proving
press

TABLE OF CONTENTS

FOREWORD

POET TS ELIOT ONCE SURMISED, "In my end is my beginning." Judy and I began teaching in the early 1970s with the goal of helping students learn, grow, and become. We found our life's work in those early days, and this project is a continuation of our early goals. Our oldest daughter Amy continues that path as an elementary teacher today.

This book is published in part to honor our daughter Susan who passed away in 2001 while a sophomore at John Glenn High School. She loved writing, and this competition was set up a couple years after her passing to celebrate her gifts by acknowledging others who share the gift of writing excellence. We wanted to do what has been called famously, "pay it forward."

In the Spring of 2003 the first competition for the Susan Awards for students attending Muskingum Valley ESC school districts was held. Dr. Barbara Hansen and Christine Wagner coordinated the program in these early years—getting information out to senior students and teachers, establishing guidelines, collecting entries, assembling panels of judges to consider student work against excellence criteria, and finally—awarding $1,000 individual prizes to not more than five students annually to those students with winning entries.

This book is an anthology of those excellent selected written pieces in many formats that have been chosen over the past twenty years. It's a book to permanently acknowledge the talents and gifts of area students by publishing some of their finest high school work. In some small way, we hope these pieces will serve as inspiration for those who follow with pieces, and the teachers who foster excellence and creativity in students. Teaching, and by extension, writing, is the gift that keeps on giving. We can enjoy reading these pieces again and again, and all proceeds from this book will be used to support Susan Awards in the future.

Lastly, thank you to all those students who took the initiative to write, had the courage to compete, and used their gifts of thinking and writing to produce these essays, poems, narratives, etc. Without you, there would be no book. Your willingness to contribute made this all possible. A special thanks to all the teachers who encouraged, nurtured, and taught these special students. Thank you also to the many judges over the years who gave of their time and expertise to consider all entries and select the best of the best. Enjoy these written pieces— each from Susan Award winners—from Susan and her family as a way to celebrate achievement in writing and teaching. Thank you.

Jim Mahoney, Judy Mahoney
Amy (Mahoney) Meyer

1. TIME
Chris Johnson, 2003

Watching the tide roll in,
Washing the sandcastles away,
Too bad the little things in life
Seldom find time to stay.

Watching the summer slip by,
Washed away by the last summer rain,
So sad the simple things in life rarely find time to remain.

Watching the snowflakes float by,
Washing the Autumn colors away,
Too bad the beautiful things in life
Barely find time to stay.

And just like everything else I've had,
You too, have gone away,
So sad the things in life you love
Can never find time to stay.

2. UNTITLED NIGHT
Rita Ray, 2003

Cool, crisp, and clean,
the tangible air nips
frostily at my soul exposed fingers,
greeting me,
meeting me,
soothing me
with lonely welcome.

The dark night
Is brilliantly lit
with an eclipsing moon,
along with whom
My friendly dark shadows dance,
with me, playing,
over lapping each other
and our other dark companions.

Continued

In the nearby sky,
the moon,
himself,
is surrounding by a few,
scattered,
distant specks of stars,
calling to them
with a burning ambient glow.

Here,
on faraway earth,
a lone rebel light
burns meanly next door,
not believing the shadowed moon
is a sufficient provider;
a single, hollow, mourning bark
is the sole protection
from the scalding light.

Surrounding me tightly,
the warm friendly air
chills me with welcome loneliness
as it coldly tugs and shoves
me and the other moon-night children
indoors to a security of fraudulent warmth.

3. SASKATCHEWAN

Kate McGuire., 2003

THE ROAD IS HARD, and soft at the same time. My eyes sting from beads of sweat and clouds of dust that we stir up as our feet scuff and pad and stamp through the trampled down dirt. I wish I were wearing slippers. Embroidered pastel satin that would get coated with the chalky dust—a good picture. But no, my sad green high tops have seen many dusty roads, and the picture they make is all too familiar. We pass an apple tree, trying to avoid the huge swarms of bees and other violent sugar addicts. It's the only thing on the horizon—the only thing that breaks the monotony of the soybean fields and the bright sun.

The tree takes me back to the times as a child when I danced through the rotting apples that lay sprinkled over the yard. I loved the smell, but so did the bees, and they scared the bejeesus outta me. They drove me inside, to the trees of books, where the apples are red gold, and the bees harmless and quaint. Many years ago, they cut my tree down, saying the bees were too much, not worth the pretty blossoms and flawed apples. I was heartbroken, outraged, forgetting how messy and material it really was.

But now we're far past the tree and completely isolated, walking without a sound. The sun is so bright that I close my eyes, trying to escape, wanting the black, but I'm flooded with bizarre and brightly colored patterns one finds on upholstery or tablecloths from decades past. They're animated—amorphous, swirling as if possessed by their own ugly color scheme.

I remember the spastic and darkly happy décor that carpeted every inch of the coach bus we rode to Florida. We speculated about bad trips, TV shows and dreams. I can still feel the rough softness of the synthetic fabric pressing against my cheek, can still hear the comforting hum of the engine as it lumbers towards paradise.

But I open my eyes and there is no sign of civilization, let alone Disneyland, just the rows and rows of soybeans. Does the presence of soybeans indicate civilization? I suspect that in nature, soybeans don't grow in straight, nicely trimmed lines. Nature may have a penchant for patterns, but she's not obsessive-compulsive. I want to come across a valley of wild soybeans, wandering and twisting into a jungle that can no more be permeated than Sleeping Beauty's castle.

4. ODE TO WINTER

Josh Eno, 2004

O winter, thou hast come again, and full,
For no more are fledgling thrushes tweeting,
Leafless boughs are silent in gust and lull,
Thou hast ended summer's time, so fleeting
And, crisply numbed, the present world hold.
For winter's dew is ice and early snow
And swallows up the morn in lasting cold,
As winter's icy breath stays water's flow.
No longer summer's hue, earth's mantle's gray,
And Leb'non's seed, all shot with green upright,
Yet under loads of wintry white do sway,
Turf too's reclothed, for winter's lawn is bright.
Yet in wonder, all's tucked in winter's bed,
Calm and quiet, cold sleeping but not dead.

5. MY BROTHERS
Josh Eno, 2004

MY BROTHERS ANNOY ME. Like many first born, I am often repulsed by their idiotic, carefree childishness. In their constant gaming, I often find them staring blankly into colorful screens, reading books while propped in odd positions, or building strange objects out of Lego pieces. Their time is spent in such unproductive ways that I recoil in disgust when I see them, zombie-like, oozing about.

And now I must share a room with them for a while. My room. Their presence is difficult. I don't necessarily mind that they have claimed whole portions of the room for themselves or that their territory is impassable, so amassed it is with articles of every shape and color. And I don't mind it so much when both of them are in there with me, so long as they are quiet. But I really do mind their weird abnormalities, their invasion of my personal space, their sickeningly innocent, childish appraisal of the world.

I am no longer a child. I have grown much in the last few years, constantly progressing to adulthood along this strange teenage journey. I have been molded as first born, conditioned to raise the family banner high, the first to embark. I have left childhood and entered a world not quite adulthood, a middle ground midway between the two.

So now I am balanced on the brink of the world, and staring into it with my limited vision I am fearful, for I see vaguely in the distance all manner of things: dark storm clouds hovering, their purpose unknown; green pastures hidden in clefts of razored rock; and oceans of prosperity lying infinitely, unreachably beyond. A thousand voices rush at me, pressing, watching, pulling, pushing. And I on the edge, no haven around me.

Here I am in this crucial period of transition in my life, and my brothers do not give me the support I crave. Indeed, they seem even not to care. They do not understand what I am going through, and they do not wish to understand. Here they are, flitting from diversion to diversion, filling their time with meaningless activity, they with nothing to do and I with everything to do, a world short of time in which to do it.

They do not help, and sometimes they even hinder. They make strange noises when I am trying to concentrate. They in their youth cannot, do not wish to understand the labors I endure in my studies. The new joys I am discovering in the opening of my mind are lost on them, and they ignore the things I have strived to achieve.

I am quick to say my brothers are a nuisance. And they are. But their moronic noises and unwanted presence have brought me a form of support that I did not want or expect but needed. In a world of noise – some theirs, some that of others, and some that of myself – they are silent in a way very profound to me. I can come away from the world of people expecting everything of me to a place where my brothers expect nothing from me. They do not nag at me, try to persuade me, or constantly remind me. Indeed, they do not even mention my future often. They show me that not everyone is after me, that there is still simple joy in childish fun, that the foundation of childhood within me is broad and able to weather great loads. What I would be if every day I did not come home to beeping gizmos and the sounds mimicked explosions I cannot think.

6. ASIAN TOURIST
Robert Evans, 2004

EVER SINCE I WAS YOUNG, I have possessed a strong attachment to the colossal heroes, incredible deeds, and the mighty gods of Greek mythology. Fulfilling one of my life's dreams, in the summer of 2003 I traveled to the birthplace of those tales and spent two weeks traipsing across the building blocks of that civilization. Somewhere in between using up 26 rolls of film, I suddenly found myself in front of very large groups of more or less total strangers singing solo – sans sheet music, serious preparation, or even a lowly pitch pipe. The most personal defining of the three of those nerve-racking, impromptu, "Oh my gosh! I can't remember the words!" experiences were the last, my short debut as a street performer.

That first appearance on the pavement stage arose from both a desire to test my courage and ability and also, more significantly, from some very poor financial planning. That is to say that my pockets contained, on the night before our transatlantic flight back home, less than three euros. Three euros, or approximately three dollars, is not much to rely upon for an entire day spent either in layover or in the atmosphere. So, drawing upon the frequent examples I had noted (and donated to) during the trip and some very ardent encouragement from other members of my tour group, I borrowed a hat, located an unoccupied spot between a tiny grocery store and small storage building on one of the three thoroughfares of the Placa district of Athens, and faced the crowd. That crowd consisted of tourists from all over the world as the Placa district is the open-air tourist shopping area of the Greek capital. I cast a final vacillating glance at the dozen fellow traveling teenagers sitting across the short distance of paving stones and, pushing aside the terror of performing so unaided in front of the hundreds of passing by, I lit into the glib baritone solo "Once in Love with Amy" from Where's Charlie. This song was given substantial backup by the noise of the city and the accelerating drumbeat of my own heart. As I worked through my repertoire, from "Mack the Knife" to "For the Longest Time" my confidence grew, and I began to relish the experience for its unique place in my musical history. I was especially heartened by the appearance of an Asian tourist who walked over, said "Very good!" and deposited two euros (which were later exchanged for a cup of orange juice) into my rented cap.

The words of that generous nameless tourist even now serve as a permanent wellspring of confidence. While not the most musically prestigious compliment I have received, those two words are one of my most treasured memories, outranked only by my family's unwavering support.

While I do not intend to take up street performance as an occupation, hobby, or even college major, the experience is still an asset to me both on and off the stage. Now, whenever I take the stage again, as a soloist at an elite choral festival or opening girls' volleyball games with the National Anthem or singing with the entire All- Ohio State Fair Youth Choir as backup on regional television, if I began to feel nervous, I remind myself of that street in ancient Athens early in the warm evening where I sang alone before tourists from dozens of nations. That mantra helps, calm, though not remove, the dreaded butterflies. By accepting that challenge, I created a footstool to even higher goals.

Sometimes this series of circumstances lead people to unique situations. I never would have thought that sitting in a John Deere tractor listening to the radio would start a chain of events that has led me to one of my proudest moments. The song that played while I sat waiting inside the cab for my father's arrival was "Thanks for the Memories," the standard of the late American icon Bob Hope. Perhaps I had heard it before or maybe the song simply drew me in, but as it began and the simple words of a pair's treasured recollections through decades of fellowship drifted through the static I listened intently, trying to capture this fascinating song in my own memory.

Several weeks later, I was in the Di Salle and Crafts building on the State Fairgrounds rehearsing songs as a member of the All-Ohio State Fair Youth Choir. That rehearsal featured our guest conductor Sarah J. Baker who was visiting to help teach the two pieces she had arranged especially for the 2003 Choir. One of those pieces was "Thanks for the Memories" and she asked if anyone knew the melody. I raised my hand but did so rather dubiously considering that the coincidental hearing on the farm was the only time before or since that I could remember having heard the tune. Mine was the only hand. Therefore, according to the logic of need, the duty of serving as the rehearsal soloist for the piece (which was rehearsed several more times that day, including several times with the entire 250 voice choir) was immediately thrust upon me until tryouts could be held.

When tryouts were conducted, I earned a rotating spot as one of the three soloists. Somehow in the pressure and fear of those first rehearsals and in practicing on my own, I had to come to enjoy the song, each day that I nervously scanned the words my desire only to give my interpretation in concert grew. Finally, the first soloist performed, and I was scheduled for the next evening. However, while marching to a concert earlier that day, the third soloist mentioned to me that his show choir (including his girlfriend) and his parents were coming to that evening performance, and he was glad I was doing that solo and not him because he would "be too nervous." I stewed over his words and decided that, while I implicitly trusted that he had spoken with no intent to try to switch spots with me, I doubted that he was truly relieved. After our exchange, I approached

Lizzie Horst, the choir's soloist coordinator, and explained the situation to her. That evening my fellow soloist gave one of the best performances of "Thanks for the Memories" that I have ever heard.

It is obvious that conventional morals dictated I act just as I did and that I should have been ashamed to still sing knowing that the performance would mean much more to Nate. Nevertheless, acting honorable does not directly translate into thinking so purely. Rather, many times, even when people do as they should, a corner of the heart remains uncooperative and obstinately holds to those dark emotions we try so hard to suppress. That night and to this day, my desire to perform the song with the incredible All-Ohio State Fair Youth Choir behind me remains just as strong (for scheduling problems I never did get to perform the song). The taint of envy that I suspected has still not appeared. Instead, I am purely elated when Nate performs the song, which has been a staple in our repertoire. To have a natural capacity for considerate action, beyond ego's (in the Freudian sense of the word) control, is an unsurpassable honor. No performance I will give, no award I win, no success I obtain is as important to me as that.

7. UNTITLED

Jesse Beauchamp, 2005

AS WE SEARCHED FOR A PARKING SPOT, I gaped at the formidable snow mountain that tickled the clouds. The sun shone brightly yet shaded the valleys with blue shadows. I couldn't believe I was going to ski on Christmas Eve at Mount Ascutney. My family had made the 14-hour trip to spend Christmas, with the rest of our family, at Grandma and Grandpa Thornburn's Vermont Inn. As a bonus, my grandparents treated the entire family to a day on the slopes: this would become the most exhilarating Christmas present I had ever received. Thirty minutes later, I strapped on my awkward moon boots and clicked into my streamline skis. The crisp mountain air: dry and pine-scented, flushed my cheeks and nose. Instantly, I was invigorated and inspired to ski the highest slope and conquer the riskiest ski jump.

"Hey Jess," my mother called out, "you gotta start on the bunny hill, then we can think about bigger ones."

My mother had obviously perceived my ambitious ogling of the summit. As I glanced to my mother's petition (the bunny slope) I was humbled. The cartoon figurines danced on the hillside: elementary kids stumbled and shuffled down the ant hill, their bottoms getting more work than their skis.

Shrugging off my aversion, my sister and I caught the next chair lift to the beginner's hill. Dangling from the chair, my heart thumped with anticipation and an inkling of fear.

"Now point your skis downhill and keep your knees steady and close together. If you go too fast, cross your skis in front of you to slow you down, Now, let's go!" my mother, a veteran skier, instructed.

I zoomed down the hill, my skis scraping the crystalline snow. The wind shipped past me tugging my hair as it went. As I descended swiftly to the bottom of the hill, my dreamy fight was interrupted. A chill was sent down my spine. How am I going to stop? Where are the brakes on these skis? Again, my heart raced, but with fear not anticipation. I gathered speed knowing I needed an exit plan. Abort! Abort! I crashed down to the snow on my side, seeing this as the only plausible plan to arrest my progress. With some maneuvering and stretching, I was back on my skis. After a few more swift flights down the bunny slope, I graduated to the intermediate slope.

On the ski lift, I saw the bulky, orange snow maintenance machines, with their notched graters and smoothers. The icy slope, the scattered pines and the Soviet-looking machinery transported me into a James Bond film. The swelling melody of James Bond theme music set the scene. As I skied off, I was pursued by gunmen on snowmobiles. The robotic report of machine gun fire echoed as I ducked to dodge the imaginary bullets. The grenades sent snow and smoke exploding into the air. With celerity and skill, I swiftly danced over jutting rocks and hard pines. I could hear the pulsing of their snowmobiles and my own pulse drumming in my ears. My sister and cousins joined the adventure armed with guns and fur parkas. All day we zoomed down the slopes weaving and crouching, evading the Soviet's imaginary gunfire.

At lunch, we replenished the energy skiing had drained.

"So does anyone want to go to the summit with me?" mom asked.

My cousin, Travis, and I were the only one's brave enough to make the adventure. Previously, on the drive to the slopes, I had gazed at the summit, having to stretch my neck just to capture its 4,000- foot elevation. Soon, we were on the chair lift on the way to the formidable peak.

We passed the bunny hill and the novice and intermediate slopes and kept climbing higher. The early morning pink aura settled in the valleys below. The phthalo blue sky was picturesque: as if an artist had just laid a vibrant watercolor wash. Dazzling white snow twinkled like a myriad of diamonds broken only by the earthy green of tall and sweeping conifers. Wooded peaks rose from the flat lands, the valleys with ensconced brooks lived in the crevices of the mountainside. A patchwork of snow-covered fields edged with scrubby hedges stretched below. Gossamer threads of chimney smoke puffed humbly out of brick farmhouses. The view was majestic in all its winter wonderland splendor: the snow whites, earthy greens, sky blues, and brick reds.

As we neared the top, the conifers became shorter and the snow drier. We reached the apex and tasted the powdery bite of fresh snow and pine. We drank in the bird's eye view of the perfect scene below. As my eyes focused onto my actual position, away from their dreamy flight over the enchanted terrain, I was warmed with a tinge of fear. The mountainside plummeted below with jagged turns and obtrusive trees. Being a novice, I knew this would be a daunting trip. Travis and I scooched our way down on our behinds cautious of any dip or sudden drop. My mother adroitly carved her way to and fro down the slope like Peak a Boo Street.

After what seemed to be an eternity, I cried out, "Land straight ahead!" like a pirate for I saw the beloved intermediate slope through the tunnel of trees. The remainder of the day was spent racing down the intermediate slope with my family.

The dying rays of the sun painted vibrant purple and warm pinkish oranges on the western sky. My family and I had been skiing since dawn: dusk signaled our return home.

Over Christmas Eve dinner, we told of our adventures and mishaps: lampooning each other in the process. Outside the snow whispered as it blanketed the hushed landscape. As I lay in my bed, my hair imbued with the odor of crisp air and powdery snow, I knew this memory would last long after the spring thaw. The flights through the clouds, the escapes from the Soviets, the panoramic view from the heavens would forever dance in my mind.

8. THE CHICKEN BATH
Douglas Wachtel, 2005

ENVISION THE SCENE: the captive struggles, clawing at the giant of a man holding her. She squawks and flails, but to no avail. The man grimaces as he lowers her slowly into... a bucket of soapy water? Is it a scene from a recent thriller movie? Not quite. I'm just recalling a scene from my years as a member of 4-H, and the unique and somewhat painful experience of bathing a chicken.

The day I acquired ten adorable day-old baby chicks, I knew I was in for a fascinating experience. Despite living in rural Appalachia, I had never had much contact with chickens, except in their processed state. My mission was to raise these birds to show quality specimens over a period of eight weeks. The chickens matured rapidly, transforming from yellow, fuzz covered, marshmallow-peep look-alikes to fat, glossy, white-feathered adults seemingly overnight. However, over the course of time their shiny white coats began to yellow with filth, and with the county fair fast approaching, I had no choice... it was bath time.

Bathing a chicken is an inexact science, due to the birds' erratic behavior and their complete abhorrence to submergence. The chicken bath consisted of four buckets, each with a different solution for each step of the process. The first contained water with a small amount of dishwashing soap to loosen dirt and manure and to clean the feathers and skin. The second held a vinegar/water rinse solution for removal of the filmy soap. The third contained a fabric softener solution intended to totally eliminate the soap and leave the feathers with a soft, smooth feel. The fourth and final bucket in the assembly line of cleanliness contained a solution of water and fabric bluing, used to remove any yellow tint from the birds' coats and provide a bright white finish to the feathers.

As I dipped my "captive" into each solution, I found it difficult to maintain a firm grip on the bird. It struggled valiantly to escape, flapping its wings about and slapping me in the face as though I had offended it personally. Its talon-like claws tore into my flesh during its panic induced rage, raking bloody wounds into my skin. But I persevered.

After the bird had been thoroughly soaked and soaped, it was wrapped in a towel and transferred to the final phase of the chicken bath ritual: the hairdryer. The bedraggled bird clucked nervously as it was subjected to a stream of warm air and roaring noise. Beginning with the downy feathers against the skin, I began to "fluff" the bird, attempting to restore it to its once-majestic state. The transformation was quite amazing to behold, a snow-white chicken as soft as a new stuffed animal.

If this truly were a movie thriller it would have a happy ending. The suffering of both bather and bathed was rewarded. In the final scene, my glossy white chicken strutted to victory and was named Reserve Grand Champion at the County Fair. A star was born! Roll credits!

9. UNTITLED
Brianne Reiss, 2005

THE FORECAST HAD CALLED for blizzard-like conditions and six to eight inches of snow. That Saturday was supposed to hold the worst snowstorm of our winter to date. Since the occasion of torrential snowfall is an unusual occurrence in our city, I was happily burrowed into an old wooden chair on the back porch, anxiously waiting for an afternoon of winter weather delight.

Nestled deep into the blue chair, my thick Carhart's and oversized jacket sheltered my body from the bone chilling wind that tore between the floor and the roof of the deck at the most unpredictable times. It was obvious that the first front of the storm had already passed, leaving a thin layer of pure white powder on everything like frosting on a cake. Glancing down the slope of the hill, the white slated fence at the bottom glowed against the dull gray background of trees. The trees were frozen, looming over the fence like a forest of icicles. Hanging precariously, each icicle reflected the sun like millions of lights shining through every nook in the branches.

Among the trees the soft clinging of wind chimes stirred the sterilized air. In the front yard a snow blower sputtered to a start and whirred rhythmically, making new space for what the storm's second front would bring. Even with layers of clothing for protection, the bite of the wind had succeeded in numbing my fingers, leaving them more like ten bumbling fools than useful appendages.

Tearing down the hill and circling around the yard, a scruffy black dog loped between the snowdrifts, ruining the seamless glassy surface of white with smudged deep ruts. With her maroon and white striped sweater barely covering her back, the dog, Abby, chased the small snowballs that were sent rolling down the hill with her every hop. It was evident that this "jump and chase" game could continue for a while, Abby appeared oblivious to anything except the crumbling snow.

As the dog continued its joyous frolicking amid the fresh snow, the sky began to clear, having just a small spattering of clouds here and there like fluffy white dandelions in a sea of blue grass. The quiet drone of the snow blower ceased, and I heard the beagles' barks echoing from within the woods. I put in a piece of Wrigley's gum and began to chew as my half-frozen jaw tingled from the forgotten exercise. Surrounded by the chilly artwork of winter, I felt out of place and uninvited- an imperfection in the sculpture.

The wind had begun to pick up again. Its slight howling added an eerie harmony to the wind chimes' gentle ting. With the addition of the wind, Abby found a new form of entertainment-leaves. Like tumbleweeds in a one-horse town, the dark leaves scooted across the ground's gloss surface, unknowingly becoming the new prey. One by one, Abby stealthily made her approach and pounced, leaving nothing but a sprinkle of crumbs in her wake. Snow began to lightly billow from the cobalt sky.

Overhead, a pair of crows cawed piercingly, a warning of the change from afternoon tranquility to the furious snow plastering due that night. As the tall trees' ghostly shadows reached across the bare canvas of snow, the sun dipped lower in the dulling sky. I stretched my hibernating legs and climbed out of my chair, whistling across the yard for Abby. As she galloped and tumbled to my side in response, the snow steadily increased. After having brushed away the ice crystals stuck in the weave of the dog's sweater, I tucked the chair back into its quiet deck corner and reached for the doorknob. The weather was declining and so was the flavor of my gum. It was time to return to the inviting warmth of my house and lock out the menacing second front of the Saturday storm.

10. GLUTINOUS GWEN
Tegan Smedley, 2005

There once was a lovely maiden named Gwen,
And her voice
Was thrice:
Chocolate, diamonds, and men.

With no reservations she indulged in all three,
But she has since
Learned the consequence.
There's a price to be paid for gluttony.

She lost her figure to the chocolate,
The diamonds stole her soul,
And in the heart of every man she met,
She left a grief-filled hole

So, Gwen went through life lonely, fat, and old,
For everyone and everything had left her,
Except the diamonds, which were forever,
But like her heart were hard and cold.

11. LONELY

Amber Mercer, 2006

I am the wind
Fearless and strong.

Invisible, yet I'm still there
I am a bare tree in a dying field.

Alone and rejected
Majestically unnoticeable.

I am the lone tear on your cheek
Rolling down
Streaking pain.

I am the kid in the back of the room
Broken pencil
Open mind
Lost heart.

12. OLD FRIEND
Carrie Guilliams, 2006

JUST AS SHE WAS from as far back as I can remember, the quaint little park of Warsaw sits in solitude. Today, I have decided to sit with her for a while. The air is bitter, but not so much as some of the Januarys she has endured in the past, I'm sure. Her trees are shivering as the piercing wind blows through their withered leaves. As my resting place, I have chosen a picnic table, the same one my grandma and I used to sit at when I was a child to watch the birds. Now the park and I can begin to make amends for lost time.

I can tell she is lonely; her creek flows unhurriedly and trickles over rocks creating a melancholy, but peaceful sound. Many of her birds have gone south, but some have remained to keep her company. They are chirping a happy melodious tune, perchance to cheer her up. The clouds shelter the sun, which gives the day little cheer. She is pleased to see me. Every so often she pushes the wind my way, blowing my hair all around, so that I know she notices me. Even though it is chilled, the breeze in my hair grants me a sense of weightlessness.

My viewing distance allows me to see the playground. She kept it just the same as I remembered from my younger years. My attention is drawn toward the swing set when a gust of wind provides the center swing with a push causing it to squeal maybe out of excitement. I hear laughter in my mind when I listen to the old chains squeaking against the hinges from which it hangs, reminding me of when my sister and I would swing on those very swings. That particular memory has been hidden within me for so long. Now that I have a remembrance of it, I desire that I could relive it just once more.

The beauty of this park is of a plain nature. She is not perfect with new equipment, but exactly as I prefer her to be. Her paths are worn, and her slides and climbing bars are rusted with age. Her courts are empty with tattered hoops, and there is a ragged net in the midst of an aged tennis court. Her fields for sporting events are vintage with blurred signs of sponsors who are, without a doubt, no longer in business. She gives me peace of mind and clears my head of all the sadness of the world. I have to ask myself now why I do not visit her more often. Maybe it is because I am pressed for time, but if I were to tell myself that, I would only be making excuses. For there is always enough time for peace and serenity which I, without a doubt, acquire form the park and all she has to offer.

Now that I have grown older and grasped that life is not all play, it is a great comfort to have the park to visit so that I can remember that life is not all work. It takes reminding for me, like many others, that even though we are no longer children, we can still feel comfort, love, and joy. The park helps me to remember joy and gives me a new perspective of happiness through serenity. The sun is setting, and I suppose that it is time for me to say farewell to my old friend. I leave quietly so that I can hear her say goodbye.

13. WALKING AT NIGHT
Mason Culp, 2006

IF I HAVE LEARNED ANYTHING about a quiet walk at night on the side of a road, it's that introspection always accompanies isolation. The act of walking through darkness may not appeal to some and may offer solace to others. Regardless, one's senses are heightened as the tempo of each breath and each step becomes the soundtrack for the particular moment. The more that I walk, the more the silence starts to din, crescendos into a pleasing audible frequency.

The melody of the night reaches a fever pitch when I kick a pebble down the darkness draped road. The sound of it skipping is like the steady pulse of a metronome ticking only three times. I listen carefully as a slight breeze passes through the trees, shaking their leaves, giving the night its rustling refrain. This refrain occurs every few seconds and coinciding with the faraway sounds of distant animals and mankind.

I find that the night is a perfect refuge for one's innermost thoughts, with the prospect of less traffic the most appealing. In fact, on this night, virtually no cars pass me by. The few that do roar quickly by. Their warm yellow lights bathe my side of the road as well as painting the adjacent side. When the car is gone, I can still hear it faintly rumbling in the background.

The road before seemingly stretches out into an endless curtain of darkness, receding into rolling hills and trees stripped bare by winter. Though, in the midst of January the weather is unusually warm. I anticipated this by dressing in a jacket, not a coat. The cool air spills into my lungs each time I breathe in and drifts slowly out with every exhale, a sigh releasing it as a mist. This wispy vapor momentarily hangs suspended in the air before becoming a part of the vast nothingness that surrounds. Every noise is captured by the air and made more crisp. The detail of concrete footsteps and snapping branches reaches my ears.

Walking further down the road, the outline of a road sign materializes in the distance, its dark silhouette growing more visible with each step. As I approach the sign, I recall that a small bridge will be to my left at nearly any moment. Without pausing, I continue walking, passing the sign and coming around the turn that brings me to the bridge. Once at the bridge, I stand and stop to admire a star-filled sky and quiet night.

I wonder about who may have traveled this road in the past and those who might in the future. I know that in a couple of months some joggers will briskly run where my feet now stand. Dressed in gray sweatshirts, pumping both legs at a rhythmic pace, they'll pass this very bridge before stopping to breathe in fresh spring air, and maybe they'll look up to the sky as I do now.

I haven't ever had to walk this road alone, and to do so fills me with several feelings at once. Instantly, I am nostalgic for a cool summer day with my brothers when we'd scramble to fight our ennui. Suddenly, I am basking in the same early morning rain that fell down nearly ten years ago when my small family decided to look for blackberries one June.

Finally, I am transported back to one summer morning so many Julys ago. In this. memory I am with my older brother just minutes after daybreak. Angry at our father, we stayed out all night and found ourselves at this bridge by dawn. I can remember everything vividly, the bitter taste of my first (and as I decided afterwards, my last) cigarette, the sight of the sun climbing over the hills, and the sounds of summer birds singing their requiem for the new day. I remember feeling complete. After taking in the beautiful birth of a Saturday, we decided to head back to the house and make amends.

As soon as I have had my share of the night sky, I glance down at my feet on the road. As my eyes refocus, the chirping birds and blue skies of yesteryear become white lines and pavement. I begin another journey and head back the way I came, knowing that this road will always take me home. No longer faced with darkness, I feel renewed with the strength of a summer day as I pass the backside of a familiar road sign.

14. BETTER DAYS

Nicole Dubosh, 2007

IT IS NEARING 6 P.M., dinnertime, and people are beginning to get hungry. Because of the dark and cold winter night it's too late to cook, but ignoring the growling of their ravished stomachs is not an option. Food is a necessity and their hunt for a satisfying and budgeted meal leads them to a diner offering a buffet. People dash into the diner that has seen better days to escape the cold biting wind and to satisfy their growing appetites. They come in and choose the empty table closest to the buffet. Their cheeks are rosy, and their hair slightly disheveled from the wind that whips a harsh reminder that winter is here. The diner is not only a place to eat tonight; it's a welcoming warm sanctuary protecting them from winter's fury. The people began to un-layer themselves, tossing their scarves of wool and thick winter coats onto the backs of the booths and chairs. They slowly slide into the red leather seats where they will soon partake in their evening feast.

I sit down on the worn, soft leather that covers the booth next to the window. The parking lot is lit dimly with the flickering streetlights and the glow from the neon sign that hangs on the door inviting customers. The leather booth displays nicks and scars that are not large enough to replace the booth but tell of its age. The light pink streaks on the seat represent the countless times people have slid across the leather to situate themselves for a meal. The solid table in front of me is a little off balance. I look at the legs of identical tables around the diner to see if they too are off balance and notice paper coasters folded into squares, wedged underneath legs in an effort to balance the surface. The top of the table has a faux marble finish that was probably glossy and realistic looking when new. The silverware sets, spotted from the loud clanging dishwasher, are wrapped in a napkin that is like sandpaper to delicate, dry winter skin. There are turned over coffee mugs resting on plates that are as dingy and stained as the scarce walls.

The tired waitress carries the stained coffee pots with thick brown handles around to each table offering the customers refills of the rich liquid gold that sloshes inside the pots. The whole gesture is polite. The waitresses wait patiently at each table for the customers who are whole heartedly engaged in conversation to notice her. As they do, they move their cups closer for the tired maids to refill and say nearly inaudible thanks. The waitresses smile softly, their eyes worn and their backs aching. They turn to the next table to begin the process again. When they come across a regular customer or a friend, they may linger to socialize or flirt with the loud and boisterous old men.

One old man sits secluded at the end of the counter. He doesn't talk to other customers or even the waitress who tends to the bar. He just sulks there slipping his coffee in a rhythm like a dipping bird. He doesn't look up. His tired eyes seem to be peering over the counter. His skin is like leather- tough, wrinkled, and worn. He has strong, deep lines around his eyes that are deep and dark. The lines remind me of rake marks made in a wet garden. His hair underneath his green cap that is soiled with grease reflects the salt and pepper shakers sitting in front of him. The old man wears dark blue slacks with a light blue button up work shirt. A pocket filled with papers, his wallet and two pens, rest upon his left breast. The shirt seems thin and tired. Perhaps that is why he keeps his red and blue flannel coat upon his shoulders. He rests directly across from the door, and gusts of the cold, bitter winter wind reach his worn skin. On his feet are tired shoes where the rubber has worn very close to the brown scuffed leather. Those shoes must have traveled many miles. They could tell rand tales about the man's journey that has led him to this diner counter and will soon lead him to wherever he rests his tired body tonight. But for now, those tired shoes rest upon the bar beneath his stool, making him lean slightly forward. His elbows and forearms rest on the countertop in front of him. He dips his neck down and sips the strong brew.

His thick, callused hands are wrapped around the warm ceramic stained mug. His callused hands, worn skin, and tired eyes reflect this man's journey. He must have been a factory worker like so many of his generation. Rising every morning, he quietly prepared for the day and shaved the stubble from his chin just like the smooth hairless face he bears today. After getting ready for work that is necessary to provide for his family, he kisses his wife, whom he has probably outlived, and his children goodbye. Today his children are probably too preoccupied or live too far away to have their father over for dinner, so he sits alone staring into his dark coffee envisioning about his past. He sips his strong brew and thinks of today. After many years of factory work, he has retired to the fate of being the old man sitting at the end of the counter alone in a timeworn diner. They have both seen better days.

15. ONLY CHILD… OLDER SISTER
Erica Martin, 2007

ON JANUARY 22, 1998, my peaceful life ended dramatically. After almost dying of boredom in a hospital waiting room, my title of "only child" was replaced with a more dubious one, "older sister".

My sister came into this world loudly, and she continues to live her life in that manner. From her dramatic concerts in the shower to her unceasing backseat chatter, Caroline is the prime example of… what I'm not. Her robust character and endless temerity forever grate against that quiet and reserved temperament, making for many interesting encounters. While Caroline will unthinkingly waltz off of the "high dive" in the dog days of summer, I have been known to dangle from the edge of that same dive, contemplating if I might be leaping into certain death. Amidst this whirlwind of personality clashing, there have been some amicable exchanges. In exchange for the silencing of her shrieks, I offered to change her diaper. In exchange for a small smile and a wiggle of tiny toes, I gave a few well-placed tickles.

Now that she's grown older, I attempt to teach her the virtues of patience and carefulness. When Caroline barrels out the door to whatever adventure awaits her outside, I make sure that she is properly equipped for the exciting escapades that she will seek, and that will find her.

In growing to love and embrace my sister, I've come to appreciate her enthusiasm for life and her free spirit. I admire that Caroline is always the first-person dancing when her favorite song comes on, and also admire that she's always more than willing to "belly up" to the feast of life. Caroline has taught me the value of letting loose every once in a while, and the importance of an unguarded heart, even if it means a few breaks along the way. I would like to think that her recklessness and my reticence balance us as sisters.

So, while I embark on the pursuit of a medical degree, I realize that when she is my age, she may pursue a career in entertainment. But as different as we are, and no matter how far we may be separated, I hope that a part of her carefree, uninhabited self will always reside in the wild side of my heart, and perhaps make me choose the road less traveled, just to see where it might lead.

16. COMMON COLD
Abe Parker, 2007

It was just a common cold; she was barely five years old.
She did as her momma told, "Take an antibody
And you will cure your common cold."

It was just a heartbreak; she was barely sixteen.
Found out he was cheating, and all her friends
Told her to stop eating, that way she might feel prettier.

It was just a pregnancy; she was so scared he would leave.
In place of his own kid, he said, "Just take these pills
And you'll cure your pregnancy."

Well, he left her anyways, she started her party days.
Every night and weekend a new guy, bottle and needles
They said would give her highs.

It was just a common gun, she was barely twenty-one,
She was scared; she started to run, wound up in an emergency room
Staring out into the blue.

Continued

It was just an HIV; it was just so hard to breathe.
Finally, she said, "Pull the cord." Twenty-nine looking fifty years old.
She died from the common cold.

People hurting people;
It's the same old mistake.
It's the one that we fake.
Here I am down
On the floor with the common cold.

17. MR. WHITE
Abe Parker, 2007

The first time I met Mr. White was summer of '04.
For fifteen bucks I'd mow his yard, sweep his back porch and his floor.
For eighty-five, Mr. White was still a child,
Smile outstretching wrinkles, and eyes coiled wild.

When I was done, I'd go inside for a water and a laugh.
He'd sing about his joy in life when living in the past.
And he would say, " I remember seventeen,
Life was still a sunrise, and minds were growing green."

Chorus

Mr. White was a handicap most of his life,
But his heart pierced right through his eyes so bright,
And the last thing that he would say before I slowly drove away,

"Don't forget to love the ones you care for while you can,
Cause money ain't worth nothing, and its faith that makes a man.
I sure appreciate you coming by
Cause it ain't every single day,
I get someone to come my way."

Continued

Across the room he'd reminisce and tell about his youth:
The time he first went fishing or the time he lost his tooth,
The time he flew far above the skies in make-believe,
His mornings in the forest and the times of all his dreams.

From his old, black wheelchair he would tell about his Ann,
How she was his first kiss and likewise, he was her first man.
And then he cried, an unexpected stringy tear
And pulled a photograph off the wall and held it near.

I guess the Japanese shot him up pretty bad.
The day he lost his leg he lost the only girl he'd have.
And I never heard him say; I never heard him tell
Me anything about the war, except for, "Boy, war is hell."

I saw him less and less now, got a job down at the store.
They took him to a nursing home, didn't see him anymore
Until the night when the nurse called with a sigh.
So, I drove down to the home, and saw the clock tick in his eyes.

"Mr., I don't know if you can hear me when I say
I love you and I wish that I could train time to obey,
But I'm saying good-bye because I just became a man And I got to move
on, now with life, and to love the most I can."

I'm sure that he was dreaming in some adolescent land
His photograph pressed to his chest and his Bible in his hands,
And then I cried a long-expected stringy tear
And I realized that I had died to all my younger years.

18. FREEDOM'S CHALLENGE
Abbigail Brothers, 2007

MUMBLING AND GRUMBLING, you hang up the phone and tell your friends you have to go home. Your parents conveniently reminded you it was nearly three in the morning, and you were supposed to be home three hours ago. Not to mention the fact that you sent two thousand text messages this month and they just got the bill. You don't see what their problem is, you let the dog out before you left. This is a common struggle teenagers face daily. As a teenager myself, I can't wait to get out on my own and be free to do as I please. Freedom is a word that means something different to everyone. For some it is the ability to worship as they please or for others simply the ability to stay out late. For me, freedom is the ability to choose. I know that I can make my own decisions, and whether I am right or wrong, I can choose for myself. Our founding fathers broke away from Great Britain so they could choose their own religion, choose their government, and choose which taxes they would pay. They died for our rights and freedoms as have many more men and women over the past two hundred years. The freedom that our forefathers fought so hard to obtain is not given to us without a price. It comes with many challenges that threaten it daily, like foreign enemies, misinformation, and limitations.

Many leaders in the world are threatened by the very idea of freedom. Free speech and thought leads to change. When governments begin to stray from the old ways of thinking, the power begins to shift from the hands of the dictator to the hands of the people. These tyrannical rulers believe that oppression and ignorance are the only ways to maintain their influence. The rulers figure out that if the general population never knows what it is like to be free, they won't want to be free. Therefore, they do not allow their people the smallest ounce of freedom and spread messages about the evils of democracy. In many cases this strategy has prevailed; many people in the world have no desire to be free. This is a concept foreign to many Americans who have lived as free people all of their lives. But to many, freedom is a distant concept that may never exist for them. They may yearn for "free" but know only that "free" means something better than where they are now. Enemies of freedom try to destroy our morale by attacking our citizens and threatening our state. We can combat these baseless attacks on our way of life by presenting ourselves as a positive force and promoting free thought in the world.

Ignorance is a serious challenge facing freedom today. In order for people to be free, to speak out about their government, and to vote for their leaders, they must be informed about the standing of their nation and the positions of their elected officials. One of the most prized freedoms in existence today is the power to run our own government. Our system of majority rule simply would not work if the citizens didn't understand the issues facing our nation. Even though it may be inconvenient to be bombarded by political ads or propaganda every time an election date is approaching, it is our civic duty to be properly informed. Even at the start of our country, our forefathers considered ignorance to be a major challenge they needed to combat, hence the formation of the Electoral College to pick the President rather than by a straight popular vote. Also, public education systems were set up strictly for the purpose of educating the masses so there could be an informed majority to make the decisions facing our newly founded country. As it was then and is now, education is the key to expunging ignorance and promoting a free society.

Freedom must have limitations. There must be a balance between the rights and freedoms of one person and what's best for the country.

People cannot do as they please. A person is free to do whatever they want as long as they don't infringe upon the rights of others. Many of the "hot topics" facing the political figures of our nation today circle around where to draw this line. For example, many religious organizations argue that abortion should be illegal because it is murder. Pro-choice groups combat this argument by saying that it is a matter of rights of the mother. Should a person be free to take the life of an unborn child or does that fetus have no choice because it is not alive? Another debate at this time, circling around wiretapping and surveillance of a suspected terrorist, is the right of the individual over the good of the nation. Is it alright for the government to "relocate" people of Middle Eastern descent as was done with the Japanese Americans in World War II? Or is it alright to assume guilt based on the color of a person's skin or the way they worship? What situations warrant extreme measures? Freedom surely cannot be boundless, but the key is finding the balance between freedom, which is by definition unrestricted, and limitations put in place to protect freedom.

Freedom is an abstract concept created as a reaction to slavery. Even its technical definition can be left open to interpretation. Freedom is what you make it whether it is taking the car out past twelve or protesting a local law with which you disagree. This is what makes it so valuable and delicate. It's not easy to obtain or maintain, but freedom is well worth the work. This ideal is fought for and dreamed about by people of many races, ethnicities, and nationalities. As Americans, we know how special we are to have the liberties that we have. Tyranny, corruption, and violence litter many governments and countries, but I can proudly say that I come from a country governed on the premise of compassion, intellect, and most importantly, freedom.

19. FALLING STAR

Megan Smith, 2007

TRUDGING OUT OF MY '95 White Taurus, I lugged my track bag and schoolbooks inside. "Star's lying down, and the fence is torn out. I don't know what's going on, but you might want to see," mom said.

Sprinting two steps at a time, I fled to slip out of my workout clothes. Taking my frustration out on my mother I hollered, "What? Why didn't you go out and see?" Scattering around for boots and warm clothes she replied defensively, "It just happened honey". I had a bad feeling in my gut. My intuition told me "It's time".

It was March and snowing. Wind tantrums made you wonder if your nose was still there. Bounding, I saw my little brother already at the scene of the crime. Dipping under an electric fence, I saw my 13-year-old bay gelding. Frantically, he struggled like a fish out of water. Instantly, I fell to my knees to comfort my best friend. His glassy eyes screamed help, sending cold chills up and down my spine. Caressing his fuzzy coat, I tried to calm and comfort him. "Call Shirley," I hollered to mom peeking out the back door.

Investigating the scene, I found that the fence had been torn far right and lay near Star. Cows spectated from a distance. Star's pasture buddy, Peaches, trotted all around us. A veteran at the age of 30 feared grazing alone.

Having evaluated, I hypothesized what happened. Because Star's brain was kept in his stomach, he got tired of cows eating "his" grass. He started chasing our little black calf, Buttercup, around. Jezebel, her mom with a severe temper accentuated with a set of horns, was only protecting her baby.

"I called Shirley...she's on her way," said mom. "When will dad be home," I questioned? "After a bit," she replied.

The horizon was tucking in the sun as snowflakes danced around us. "It's ok Star I'm here. It's ok, relax. Everything's going to be ok." I said. The dogs started barking and, in the distance, I heard the tinking of gravel against metal. Shirley was here.

She came briskly and started examining. Star's nostrils flared as his exhale got deeper by the second. Clasping his rear right flank, she tested its reflex. "Let's try and stand him up. He can't sit down like this. Star needs to get up so he can breathe." she said.

"Should I call a vet," mom asked? "Yes," I snapped. "Now, HURRY." The throttle of my father's car could be heard coming up Butcherknife Road. "Let's make him get up," said Shirley.

"Come on Star... don't give up on me... I know you can do it... come on," we encouraged. Dad came up to my side and together we rolled him over in a sitting position and from there he stumbled to his feet. Snorting with wide eyes, Star walked with a peg leg. Peaches pranced and whinnied wildly around us. Her instigation caused Star to freak out. Being a stubborn character made Star hard to control on a good day, so controlling him while he was freaking out was nearly impossible.

"He probably just needs it put back in place. I don't know if you've ever seen one have it done but it's the weirdest thing. We had one. The vet came out tapped it a certain way and he was fine." Dad said.

Star's right rear failed to catch his weight and he fell slowly, but hard, like a barrel. Instantly, we fell to our knees. Star wheezed as his grass gut moved in and out. "Call the vet," I cried. "NOW."

Again, we tried to get Star to sit up. He refused. The pain was more than he could bear. I massaged him behind the ears because I knew it would relax him. Snowflakes were sticking to his coat. I then stroked his satin muzzle, his whiskers tickling me. As I did, his breath warming my hands.

"The vet on call at Dr. Martin's is taking care of a cow and the soonest one can be here is in two hours," Mom informed, seemingly hours later. "So, call another vet," I hollered. Star's breathing was slowing dramatically. His movement was almost non-existent. His eyes were becoming cloudy and centered. I knew he was starting to leave us. "Dad," I cried. He put his ear to Star's chest. Then, he began thrusting with both hands to perform CPR.

"NO...NO" my dad repeated turning and walking away. Tears were in his eyes. I looked in disbelief. Shirley came to my side and threw her arms around me. "I'm so sorry Megan," she said crying.

Sharp pains entered my chest as the realization set in. For several minutes I lay crying hysterically like a mourning mother attached to the body of a child's corpse. I failed to accept the fact that Star was gone. I felt that if I just held onto him as tight as I could, he would come back.

My dad knelt beside me saying, "He was a good horse... you couldn't have asked for a better horse." Filled with numbness I sat up. My glasses were fogged and smeared, and my outline was traced on Star's barrel by snowflakes.

Unconsciously, I moped to the house. "Honey, I'm so sorry we'll get you another horse," said Mom tenderly. "I don't want another horse," I said without emotion. Mom hugged me and as much as I felt like crying, I couldn't. NO ONE got it. Star was more than a horse.

In Mom's arms, my mind wandered. I went back to that day I first rode on my own, petrified of horses. Overcoming my fear, I fell in love. Saving babysitting and birthday money for two years, I finally had enough for the horse of my dreams. I remembered the first time I met Star, and my dad knew he was the one. I thought back to the day I saddled up and rode Peaches all on my own- a test my dad gave to make sure I was ready.

The day I sat with my brothers in the living room and heard mom tell us with tears she was diagnosed with cancer echoed in my ear. And how, through an unselfish act of love, she gave me the best gift I had ever gotten. She knew I needed it and had earned a horse.

Mom squeezed and released me. Star became my best friend and a horse of hope. Star was my way of coping with my mom's illness and new-found responsibilities. He was a symbol of hope, a journey, and a dream that I made a reality.

Picking up the phone I dialed my uncle. "Mitch… ok well tell him Star passed and I wanted him to help me bury him…ok…thanks…bye."

I stayed inside until my dad came back with the tractor. I insisted on burying him that night. The snow was falling heavily. I didn't want him to get cold. It was the only small comfort I had.

We crept up the gravel road to a clearing in the woods bordered by hay fields. "You can stay in the truck. It's going to take me a while," dad said.

Snow flickered in the headlights. Dad kept digging and digging with a big yellow arm that was attached to the back of the tractor. Finally, dad and Mitch got cold and decided to warm up in the car next to me in silence.

Dad was finished. Inside, I took a long cleansing shower. Even though I felt better I still felt like I was dying. I headed to bed hoping that I would wake up and it would all go back to normal. I would wake up sweating and disoriented and it would all be just a bad dream. "Megan… I buried him facing your window," dad said as I trudged up the stairs. Unable to cry and exhausted, I slept.

20. WHO SAYS GIRLS CAN'T HUNT?

Megan Smith, 2007

DARK RED AND BROWN LEAVES crackled and snapped. The sun was starting to descend as my teacher, Mr. Skinner, and I strode smoothly among the edges of a soybean field. Something in the air whispered to me and I envisioned my shot on a deer. Its clarity caused me to shiver. Today was the day.

At a maple tree bordering the woods we stopped. Mr. Skinner stretched up the ladder with our bows and aids. He quietly came down to spot my climbing. I clenched my fists tight as my muscles stretched and metal tinked beneath my feet. Tucking my head beneath the shooting rail, I slipped into what would be my seat until dark. Once situated, I could see a gravel road on my left and a house in progress across the field. The areas I was most concerned with resided at my right and rear. This is where my opportunity would be. No branches were in sight that would falter the arrow from its intended flight.

Mr. Skinner explained to me the patterns that the deer would most likely follow, a path that led straight to the soybean field beside the tree in which we were perched. He told me to imagine scenarios. This way I would be mentally prepared. We sat scanning the wood line. Nothing. We were a vision of camo. From the holey boots of my brothers to Mr. Skinner's mask and hat, nothing could be seen but my eyes...scanning.

Mr. Skinner looked like an owl searching the ground below and a vibe of wisdom could be felt. Robins and blue jays sang and gathered beneath on brush white gray squirrels scurried around after nuts. It was September 30th and gorgeous! The lively calmness of the woods was more than therapeutic. It was a connection; unlike anything I've ever known.

I began to search with new eyes. The horizon was filled with bare trees…there, a doe. Gently, I nudged my teacher. "There's a doe!" I said. His body shivered wildly with anticipation. He looked through his binoculars and then range finder, which read eighty yards. The doe looked closer than she really was, but it was too far for a shot. Our goal was to be patient and possibly this young doe would come closer. If nothing else, the doe could serve as a decoy to lure bucks to the field. The trouble was, the sun slid behind us as our decoy grazed carelessly. A breeze came fanning past as the sun ticked away.

There! Another crept out into the open. Hungry anticipation came over me. I was beginning to fidget. Now Skinner informed me that our new arrival was a young bunk and one we should pass up. He ate cautiously with the doe. Their heads paced up and down like oil wells.

Time was fading. A rustle echoed into the woods. Could it be? Yes, another buck peeked out from the right where the doe was. The small buck startled when he heard the brush rustling from behind him. Obviously frustrated, the new arrival glided toward the other. They traveled to a mound of deadwood 40 yards away where the two of them charged at each other, like I had seen in Bambi. A front row seat. Skinner whispered, "A 6-point buck." Though our faces were concealed we could still see the joy in each other's eyes.

After being rammed several times by the 6-point, the button buck decided he had enough and fled. The 6-pointer beamed with pride and strutted onward. I couldn't believe he was moving toward us. My teacher was going crazy. I had never seen him shale or lose control of breathing like he did. "Do you want a buck?… You can take him if you want" he whispered confidently. "Stand up."

I kept thinking of all the people who told me I couldn't-all the guys my age, especially. "Get a buck...yeah right!" they would say. I took off the camo gloves he had given me and stood up. My arrow was nocked. "Get ready to draw," he said. The buck kept pace. He stood broadside and turned to face us. "Draw back," he said. I pulled the bow to fit my body. Mr. Skinner made a call I never heard before: "Mahaa" The buck halted tensely. Skinner's nervous voice encouraged me, saying, "Take the shot... pin right behind the shoulder...17 yards." I would have except my sight pins were aimed at the trees. I hesitated. My mind went blank. "Shoot." I told my finger. I gently placed it on my release. I dropped my bow arm and settled to where I could see the deer's body through the sight window. I focused my yellow pin behind the deer's shoulder and unconsciously squeezed my back muscles-thunk. My arrow flung forward. Whack! The buck bound through the forest. This was the longest minute of our lives.

Everything seemed so surreal. I stood, waiting, and trying to make sure I wasn't dreaming. Skinner squeezed my legs and he let out a deep sigh of relief. "You did awesome." He said.

I had to sit down. "Did I hit him?" I asked. Now I was the one quivering, my heart pounding. "Yes, awesome shot." I kept asking if he was sure.

We waited until dark settled in, watching the oblivious doe in the field trying to calm down. Skinner descended swiftly and I shimmied down behind him. We briskly walked back to the house. We celebrated with a pop and deer snack sticks. This was the biggest smile I had ever seen on my teacher's face, and I ever felt on mine.

We undisguised ourselves and grabbed a flashlight. We quickly moved to the point of our encounter to search for traces of blood. I felt like I was part of CSI Miami. We couldn't find the arrow or any traces of blood.

"Blood," he said. I was beginning to feel more confident, but the mystery still loomed. Did I hit him? The trail led us to a tree with blood and a broken piece of my arrow below it. The blood flowed consistently on the path across a creek. Suddenly the blood became scarce. We crept from one spot to the next, scanning leaves and trees for blood. What was that? I would have sworn that I heard something on the top of the hill.

"Go with the flow" he kept telling me. I kept saying, "If I was a deer, where would I run?" We tried several possibilities before tracing out way along a bank and at the corner of the bend in the road, we found money. I jiggled the light in front as we inched our way up a hill. Just when we thought we couldn't find any more there he lay, right in front of us, over a barbed wire fence.

I couldn't believe it- a perfect shot. I bent down, picking his head up by the antlers, a gesture I saw most often on my brothers' hunting movies. I was the first in my entire family to harvest a deer with a bow, I was told by boys my ages I would "… never get a deer or a buck," or a sarcastic, "Yeah right." So many people told me I couldn't. Even if my deer wasn't the "Monster or trophy buck" I had dreamed about, I was excited by the fact that I had something to look forward to. With a quivering hand, I filled out my temporary deer permit.

Our friend, "Tonto", showed up looking for a track job and soon after two other close friends joined. Together we field dressed and moved the deer from the woods. Once at the house, I posed for a thousand different pictures for my friends. We placed plastic in the back of my 1995 white Taurus and headed down the road to permanently tag my trophy at our local guns and archery shop.

When we got there, they were just as excited as I was and wanted to hear all about my experience. They even took a picture for their "brag board" and requested a better one once they were developed.

Upon returning home, we hung the deer in the garage where it aged for two days. Three friends and my little brother, who had to see to believe, helped me with processing. We caped the hide and donated it to our friendly taxidermist. Then we cut the meat into steaks and burger. Our plan is to make my favorite, deer jerky. Music played in the background while I learned about the different cuts of meat and how to properly butcher a deer. Working with friends made this experience much more enjoyable.

Later that week, I cooked back straps for my family. This is the first time my family has had venison for dinner and now we're hooked. My mom, who hates meat, cooked venison for the first time even though my brothers have harvested many. While eating, she said "Megan, do you think you can take me crossbow hunting?"

21. I LOST MYSELF
BETWEEN THE LINES
Cassandra Marsh, 2008

READING HAS BEEN A HUGE PART of my life as far back as I can recall. I'm unable to recollect any memories of actually learning to read, but I still have one of the first books I read in in all its worn and torn splendor, "Where's Spot?" As a child, I was rather introverted, and books always provided me company. I believe Harvard president Charles W. Eliot said it best in his quote, "Books are the quietest and most constant of friends; they are the most accessible and wisest of councilors, and the most patient of teachers." Reading has always had its significance in my life: in academics, in the simple enjoyment of it, and in combination of the two in studying things I love.

From the time when I was a young girl, barely old enough to hold a pencil, to this, my senior year, it's been drilled over and over into my conscience how extremely vital academics are in one's life. It's already an inevitable fact, even at the kindergarten level, considering that one spends eight hours a day, five days a week, and nine months a year in school. Though I realize that some, possibly many, students care very little about their studies. I'd consider such a disposition toward my academics absurd. I can't trace it back to a certain incident or person instilling this attitude; I can only say that it's been there for as long as I can remember. Colleges and career paths have always swirled around in the front of my mind and every choice I make in life is somehow affected by it. The standards I've held myself to are always high, reflecting whatever future I happened to lay out for myself at the time. I spent a good portion of middle school striving for those perfect grades because I talked myself into going to Harvard and becoming a lawyer, knowing full well that I'd need a hefty academic scholarship to attend and just how rare they were.

Though academic reading can occasionally be pleasant, it's reading for the pure entertainment of it that I find truly satisfying. Though I've lived a very happy and healthy life that I wouldn't change for anything, I'll admit that my family never has had all that much when it came to economic matters. We've never been without a roof over our heads, food on the table, or clothes on our backs, but we've also never had a real vacation because we just don't have the financial resources. In lieu of travelling to Myrtle Beach, Disneyland, or any other place that I knew everybody else vacationed at, I gravitated towards books. I would get lost in one book after another, letting it engulf my reality for the time I was with it. In a matter of hours, I could travel across the world, across time, and even across the lives of other people. Books became a gateway into worlds exciting and filled with adventure, and I never wanted to be without that. In elementary school I can recall filling my backpack with book upon book until it was so full that I had trouble even lifting it. I eventually made it to school every day and began my morning ritual of stacking the books on my desk. It was a definite hindrance in regard to the amount of space I had to do actual work, but that never mattered to me. As long as I could reach over at any time and be thrown into a world of science fiction in a Goosebumps book or hang on every suspenseful twist and turn of a great mystery, any difficulty was well worth it.

Although while I was younger, I kept reading for academics and reading for enjoyment two completely separate ideas in my head, as I grew up, I realized that combining the two gave me the best of both. It never occurred to me that the two could be mutual until I had to write an editorial for my media productions class. As I researched the "War on Christmas", a topic that I found of great interest, I began reading more and more articles about it, long after I finished my editorial. I suddenly recognized that I was studying something, not for school, but simply because I enjoyed it. Ever since, I have continued to read and study subjects outside of the required academics. Anytime something catches my eye and I want to learn more about it, I do. With the worldwide web at my fingertips, all it takes is a few strokes of the keyboard and I can have more web pages concerning a subject than I could ever read. One of the best examples of this is my interest in web development. It began with the simple wondering of what "HTML," an acronym I randomly came across was, and it quickly became almost another school subject for me. I searched and read anything and everything that explained the ins and outs of designing web pages, and I became so engrossed in it that I've decided to make it my career.

As I've grown older, I've found myself wanting to wrap the comfort of a good book around me less and less. I've become more social and involved in so many activities that I hardly have time to read for school, much less for entertainment. Occasionally I do find the time to read a book, such as Harry Potter books, and still experience the same submersion into its fictional reality, but it's nothing compared to my earlier years. With a full class schedule, however, I have no doubt that I'll be reading plenty of textbooks this year. Though lately I've been focusing on the magnitude of reading in regard to my academics, reading will also forever be important to me for the entertainment and studying things I enjoy as well.

22. UNTITLED
Chelsea Adams , 2008

The lamplight by my bedside flickers dim.
These years of working past the light of day
Have taken nearly all my sight away,
So now I turn my eyes to views within.

For there lie scenes which memory can recall
The dresses of the lady trees in fall,
Or silver sheets of frost on winter's wing,
Some smile, honest, true, and welcoming.

Could I forget the billowed cloaks of hills?
The pastures where we walked with quiet thoughts
Of love, a love in Beauty's likeness wrought,
And made of simple joys, angelic thrills?

Could I forget the painted gate of white
Which stands a quiet sentry in the night
Outside our windowsill of hand-worked wood—
Or, was it stone in which the thin panes stood?

And white—was this the color on the gate?
Or was it traced with reddish hue, or grey?
And did those hills all gently roll away,
Or were they sharper mountains, cliffs innate?

Continued

I fret, for now the pictures, all but gone,
Have melded to a single stew of dawn.
Yet rising from the darkness in my mind—
A fiery orb of wisdom, which I bind—

Within the deepest oceans of my soul.
And there, at anchor, sitting tranquilly,
It waits. It calls and beckons me
To hear the message which would make me whole:

The eyes know but a trace of Beauty's hand,
Her better half within the heart of man
And one who gives his sight will see, in time,
For Beauty makes his darkened heart to shine.

23. WHAT AN ENTRANCE
Shecky Baptista, 2008

MY BIRTH—AN EARTH-SHAKING EXPERIENCE.

Conditions: An earthquake occurred
during the time of my birth.
Date: July 16, 1990
Place: Manila, Philippines

I.

"PUSH! PUSH! You have to wake up and push! You can sleep later. Right now, you have to push! Push... Push..."

It is tight. It is dark. I see light. I am afraid. I want to stay warm. Stop squeezing me out. I don't want to leave. Don't push! Please don't push! I want to stay. I'm not safe out there! No! The light! I miss the dark. It is too bright. My eyes burn. Breathe? Too much white. Too many faces. I close my eyes. Breathe. I am scared. Breathe. Big, warm hands place me in a clear box. The walls are cold. I am screaming. Too much light! Too much noise! Shaking, shaking, shaking. Stop shaking! Too much shaking! Shiny objects fall, one by one. Crash! Tiny sparkles fall. White. White. So much white. White. White... Black! It is coming closer. Closer. Closer. Now it is above me, covering me. It is covering the light. Dark. Dark. Dark. I am safe.

II.

I enter into an unknown world, only to find chaos and destruction. I am ignorant to the violent force threatening my new existence. My young, undeveloped mind cannot grasp the idea of the intensity and devastation unfolding all around me. The foundations shake beneath me as I lay in an open box. Where I am surrounded by clear walls. I am trapped, confused, and frightened. Dust and plaster from the ceiling continue to fill my encasement. Through the glass walls, I see people running in all directions. I feel their warm bodies against my confining walls. I hear their screams of terror and desperation. I hear their feet stomping around me. I sense the fear and tension hovering all around me. Despite all the turmoil and my own fears, I remain enclosed in my clear box, unable to do anything. I feel invisible. I feel vulnerable. I feel exposed. I feel lost amidst a sea of white doctor coats and nurse uniforms.

I see a man in a black uniform. His eyes dart from one end of the room to the other. We make eye contact. His face has a look of alarm, but his eyes show compassion. He makes his way towards me, as he dodges bodies pushing against him and falling debris. He is now above me. He places his body over me and shields me from the falling debris. I must be crying because I can hear him humming a song. I direct my eyes toward the shiny badge on his chest. I can see it glisten as he moves. All I want to do is touch it. I want to hold it. How does it feel? Is it hot? Is it cold?

III.

My mother delivered me when the massive earthquake began, therefore she was unable to protect me. Although my mother did not see the sheriff's act of kindness, the nurses informed my mother of his courageous deed. My mother not only named me after Shecky Sheriff to signify my earth-shaking birth, but also to honor the sheriff. I don't know why the sheriff chose to risk his life for me. Maybe it was because of his duty to serve, honor, and protect. I often wonder what was going on in his mind. Did he hesitate or contemplate the reasons why he saved me? During that split moment of indecisiveness, did our lives lie in the balance? Maybe he thought of his own daughter; he would have wanted someone to protect her if he were not able. I felt safe in the presence of a stranger. Would I have survived without him? It is possible that I would have survived without him, but the fact is that I did survive, and he protected me.

24. HOW NOT TO DIE AT A ROCK CONCERT
Ellen Shipitalo, 2008

IN MY SEVENTEEN YEARS of existence, there have only been two times when I have feared for my life. One of them occurred at the age of five, when I was lost at a shopping mall. The other was at a rock concert that got out of hand. Oh, you may think that most rock concerts are filled with awestruck fans and docile potheads but try thinking a little harder. One of those awestruck fans might mash your face into a sticky pulp to catch a highly prized drumstick that was thrown into the crowd by his or her favorite band member. And if you think that pothead is really "docile," think again.

These people can be found in a "mosh pit" along with hundreds of other music fans who are looking for an invigorating and somewhat primal experience. A mosh pit defined by *Encarta Dictionary* as an area in front of the stage at a rock concert where people dance wildly and energetically. I prefer to describe it to you as a group of animalistic, oftentimes violent concertgoers with only one thing on their head-banging mind: "get as close to the stage as possible." Rock concert mosh pits can be some of the most dangerous and exhilarating places on earth, and you should know a thing or two about them before participating in one.

Before attending a rock concert where there will be moshing, a few preparations must be made to make your experience enjoyable and safe. To stay as safe as possible in a mosh pit, there are two golden rules that you and everyone around you should follow for the duration of the concert.

The first rule is that if you are pushed, you should always push back. This helps keep the pit moving, and to prevent you and people around you from being knocked over. The second rule is that if someone near you falls down, it is important to help the person up to prevent him or her from being trampled.

On the day of the concert, your look must be practical, yet unique. Don't go into a mosh pit in only underwear, suspenders, and flip-flops. That look is overdone, and plus, open-toed shoes are not very amusing when the sweaty, shirtless man next to you is proudly sporting cowboy boots. The typical outfit worn is a black t-shirt, jeans, and comfortable shoes. Also, on the day of the event, make sure you drink plenty of water. Moshing is as much or more physical than any sporting event, and it is best to stay hydrated to prevent extreme exhaustion or fainting.

Once you arrive at the event, it becomes your sole purpose to get as close to the stage as possible, because a great view of the show always makes the concert more enjoyable. Before entering the mass of teeming, sweating bodies in from of you, try to identify the best route to the front. Avoid sections where it looks as if people are struggling for air, and also avoid particularly violent areas where hairy, animalistic men appear to be fighting like a pack of hyenas over an antelope carcass. Once you have your plan of attack, begin moving. As you progress, tap other concertgoers lightly on the shoulder to let them know that you intend to squeeze past them. Generally, they will be pretty cooperative and should make room for you. As you go deeper and deeper, the bodies will get thicker and thicker, and the spaces will get smaller. Just continue tapping shoulders, and a slight shove may become necessary in cases of people who cannot move or refuse to let you pass.

If you reach a point where you feel you cannot go any deeper into the pit, you should start moshing with the crowd. The other moshers will generally move aggressively with the music, and it is important that you let their actions influence your own. For example, if the group of skinny, shaggy-haired skateboarders next to you suddenly begin shifting to the right, you should either shift with them or push them forcefully out of your way. If you do not react quickly enough, you will be knocked over.

An additional feature present in most mosh pits is crowd-surfing. Crowd-surfers are regular concertgoers who have managed to climb to the top of the mosh pit and are supported by the hand of moshers below them. If you suddenly feel overcome with the urge to surf, tap the shoulder of a tall, strong individual (choose wisely) and he or she will lace his or her fingers and launch you up into the middle of the crowd, crushing the unfortunate and unsuspecting people in the general vicinity of your body and flailing limbs. If you choose not to leave your body at the mercy of strangers' hands beneath you, be aware of other crowd-surfers overhead for the duration of the concert. If you feel you are too weak to support surfers, position yourself near large, muscular, and experienced concertgoers who can move crowd-surfers along quickly. It is against the golden rules of moshing to let a surfer drop to the ground, but it will happen from time to time. Many injuries stem from these falls, but surfing is an incredibly thrilling experience that is well worth the injuries.

If you do not leave a rock concert mosh pit bruised, bloody, sweating, injured, and exhausted, you did not make the most of your moshing experience. But if you come out of a pit feeling as if you just endured a car accident, congratulate yourself. The event you just survived is the closest to a mass riot that most people will ever get. The pure adrenaline residing in your system from a rock concert can last for days, and you will definitely get a familiar feeling of exhilaration each time you tell your story to your friends.

25. BLUE
Lydia Gosnell, 2009

THEY SAY THAT THE FIRST COLOR the mind forgets is blue. I wish every day for this to be a lie. Still, I can feel the images fly from my mind like blossoms in the fierce winds of a storm. I cling to those I have left, to your eyes piercing through the soft darkness, and to the sound of your haunting whispers. Thankfully, I remember that first night.

I hate parties, I always have. They hold such promise when talked about and laughed over, and afterward, everyone remembers what good times the gang had together so that those who missed the fun can regret that they didn't slip out of their dark homes to the bright explosions of laughter. I have yet to experience the things that make parties wonderful. They seem to hold such a promise of joy; yet when I arrive, I inevitably find myself curled up in some far-off corner attempting to read a novel in the hazy din of apparent amusement.

That night, I forgot a novel. Music that I had never enjoyed or figured out how to stand blasted my brain as I wandered about looking for some bit of literary material. There weren't any.

Somewhere in that modest, cookie cutter mansion was reported to be a library. It must've been secretly tucked away behind the walls spartanly hung with "modern" artwork. After wandering in the dark with the lights flashing deliriously, I stumbled upon a sliding glass door out to a manicured back lawn. The moon was full and the other houses in the neighborhood still waited for those pretending to be rich enough to buy them.

With a giddy imagination, I wandered out into the blue world, only to be moderately disturbed by the pounding bass lines down the hall. A faint breeze blew through my thin hair and around my crinoline-puffed skirt. High above the foolish and petty world, deep purple clouds blew around the moon, hiding the stars and giving the sky an eerie cast. It was in weather like this that the phantoms of childhood used to ride, cackling unto the world and terrifying it to bed.

Though the wind was warm, I shivered. The empty night seemed a thousand times more intriguing than the polluted party.

"What do you think?"

I turned to see you there, leaning against a perfectly sculpted maple tree in the shadow of the moonlight. Your hair seemed nearly white. It looked like moonlight. Your pale teal shirt sleeves were rolled up aimlessly and though you wore black dress pants, your feet were bare.

You looked out of place among the perfection and the planning of the house's owner, though you made a perfect picture. Perfect in your imperfection.

"Huh?"

I admit I was taken aback. I was supposed to be alone, with my fantasies.

"What do you think?"

You didn't sound frustrated in the least bit. I shrugged. Confessing my picture of the world wasn't a normal practice.

"It's a beautiful landscape."

A smile played on your lips, and you stood up and took a few steps.

"Really?"

You weren't suave like the others at those parties. In my experience, it was the boys who flirted shamelessly, not the girls, yet you just said what you thought, and brightness flittered in your face. I nodded and then paused.

"I wish it was the way it used to be, not chopped up and left sparse. Did you know there used to be a forest here? I imagine it was simply breathtaking in the moonlight."

You gazed around at the poor excuse for natural vegetation with a familiar sadness on your face. I'd seen that look on my face as I drove past a modern building where once stood a wild and mysterious lot.

"It was."

And you turned your face back toward me, I saw your eyes for the first time. Two haunting, pale blue lanterns locked on my own. Fire hung behind them, causing them to blaze with strange warmth. I suddenly felt unwelcome, an intruder in your own special world.

"I'll just go back inside now."

I walked briskly toward the sliding glass door.

"Do you really want to?"

The honest question pulled me around, away from the door. I shook my head.

"I hate parties."

And then I found myself laughing at the absurdity of the whole situation. You laughed too. Crystal music of a thousand starlit nights washed over my heart.

"I didn't used to."

It made you sad to say this.

"Parties used to be a mystery world where people who knew each other well could suddenly see each other in a completely different way. And light used to fill everything. And the music used to be just as much for the nights as for the pleasure of the partygoers. Now the parties are among strangers, in the darkness, with contempt for the wonder of the night."

I stayed by the door, unable to move. You said exactly what I thought about parties. That was why I hated them. What wonder there once was, had been replaced with a poor substitution.

"Esther!"

I felt jerked out of the moonlight when the voice called from the hallway. I didn't want to move. I didn't want to leave. I just wanted to stay there looking at you. But things don't work out that way.

"That's my ride."

I whispered this. And I could almost see the words float out of my mouth on the moonlight to your ears. You nodded, but as I opened the glass door, your voice called me back.

"Your name is Esther?"

I looked back and nodded. A joyful smile sprang onto your face.

"What's your name?"

I had to know.

"Blue."

With that, you walked to the other side of the house, and I was forced to wander back into the false world of strobe lights and badly written music.

26. MY SPLENDOR IN THE GRASS
Kaitlyn Smith, 2010

MY WHOLE LIFE, that I can remember, has been spent growing up on a farm. Though it is not very large in comparison to others in Ohio, it is of good size with a barn, pond, and rustic log cabin. My home is of a dark wood with horizontal logs three times as wide as a grown man's bicep, and it is complete with exposed coarse and irregular logs which were hand hewed. The barn which has held many games and imaginings is of a considerably lighter color and has rough, uneven boards running vertically. There are large gaps between the boards from weathering in, like my home, the roof is of a dark Forest Green. The pond is about a football field away from my home. Now, you must pass through horse and cow pastures but "back then" it was all open fields. (It was a field with rolling hills, in which you might see a character from *Little House on the Prairie* run through)

My best friends that shared all of my childhood memories included Jamie, and my younger brother, Hunter. Hunter is a very stubborn person. He is athletic and smart but also very shy and cares a great deal about what other people think about him. Jamie lived "up the hill" as we liked to call it.

Jamie was, and still is, a very artistic person. She was always drawing and reading. I wished to emulate her so badly. This emulation led to our library. Every day we will go to each other's bookshelves and borrow something. We would each catalog it in our own notebooks and return the books when finished. Jamie also believed in fairies. So much so that she had me, as well as herself, convinced that they really did exist. In the mornings or late into the evenings we would walk to each other's houses and we would see the frost and dew. When these types of precipitation formed in the cobwebs, they looked like tiny cities or kingdoms. The tall grass and cobwebs were the fairies' home, and we would inspect almost every single one on our path. We never saw a trace of a fairy, but it never stopped us from believing. This was one of the first things I really fixated on, and it was so fascinating.

One very hot summer the chickens had gotten very excited. They were running around and when they were done, not all of them drank water. One got overheated and the small animal died. Jamie and I also went to the same Catholic Church. Jamie was always more religiously aware, and she insisted on praying for the chicken. There we sat on top of the red plastic slide bowing our heads and praying for the chicken. It might have had a name at the time, but it has now escaped me. I saw that day how important everything and everyone is. I gained more of an appreciation for life by praying for that chicken than for the eggs that it provided me. I saw how much life means and how actual reflection will help to make something's value stand out.

When Jamie wasn't around to play, or had to complete the dreaded chores, my brother and I had many adventures. We would travel down to the pond and sink into the mud. Our pond did not fill up easily and often looked like a giant crater with an extremely large puddle at the bottom of it.

Similarly, we would venture out into our 40 acres of woods. It was always thick and green, smelling of earth. The journey seemed very long even though we were always a yell and an echo away from our home, made of the same earth we were playing in. While in the woods, we would find a part of the Creek that ran straight through our land, and we went on earth the cold flat rocks that covered its bottom. Sometimes we would unearth crawdads and salamanders which Hunter would capture and take to the house to study for days.

When my dad began constructing our family's barn it became a hazardous playground for my brother and me. We would play in the skeleton of the building smelling of fresh wood and newly moved earth. The sunlight often streamed through the boards or "ribs" of the building. It made our skeleton seem happy and full of the promise of a complete building. Hunter was often a horse, and I was the brave cowgirl owning a ranch on my own. We would put on our cowboy hats and wear the gear of our characters.

When no one was available to play with, or I felt independent, I was the opposite of a cowgirl, an Indian. My grandmother made me a Pocahontas outfit because of my obsession with the Disney movie. I would wear that garment and traipse around seeking out enemies. My mother kept a large garden filled with corn and sunflowers and I would often hide amongst the tall stalks hiding and watching. I loved the earth between my feet and the smell of pure plants and vegetables surrounding me. My father helped me to create a large teepee out of genuine river birch and a tarp. I would play in the teepee until boredom set in, and then I would seek another occupation with my Longbow.

While reflecting upon my childhood I can honestly say that I had some truly wonderful adventures. I created, with my brother and Jamie, a world in which I learned and grew in knowledge and relationships with others. I grew up patient and listening to others. My experience allowed me to be a child with a vivid imagination, while I learn things about my life and skills to help me forever. I hope I will carry my childhood with me forever and keep my mind what Pablo Picasso once said; "every child is an artist, the problem is how to remain an artist once he grows up."

27. WHO I AM
Karlie Collins, 2011

A COLLEGE ESSAY is supposed to be about you. If I pulled your essence out and put it on this paper, what would it say?"

Who am I? One of life's biggest questions, and it was posed to me five minutes before lunch. I stared dumbly back at my English teacher and my mouth, which usually spit words out at rapid fire, was silent.

If you asked a hundred different people who I was, you would get a hundred different answers. My father would tell you that I am an athlete, and the basketball that has taken up permanent residence in my jeep could attest to that. My best friend would tell you that I am a nerd but considering that I can beat any boy at the game *Super Smash Brothers*, I would take that as a compliment. My mother would tell you that that I am a slob (admittedly, my room does look like it was attacked by the love child of a hurricane and a tornado).

But there are things about me that even the closest to me do not know. Like how every time I look at the night sky, I am completely entranced. Studying astronomy is one of my greatest ambitions. Or how writing a novel is at the very top of my bucket list. I always have a dozen ideas in my head, and a few hundred-word documents saved in a secret file. If you asked what my favorite book was, my father might guess the well-worn copy of *Ender's Game* on the nightstand by my bed. If you asked me the same question, I would stare hopelessly at my giant bookshelf, feeling confused as a mother asked to pick her favorite child.

But who am I? I am a tangled mess of contradictions and good intentions, with a few healthy doses of sarcasm thrown in. I label all my CDs with movie quotes. I have actually watched the History Channel for no reason other than curiosity. I have been known to stay up all night, huddled outside with a blanket and a constellation book, trying to match the pictures with the stars. I will run three miles without complaint, but if given the choice between sprinting a hundred yards or having a leg amputated, I would respond, "so, I'm allowed to replace this with a prosthetic, right?" as I climbed onto the operating table.

Writing this essay has shown me something— I do not have a clue who I am. But I'm not worried. Judging by what I know so far, I'd say I sound like a pretty interesting person.

28. THE MAGIC PURSE
Jazmin Frank, 2011

Head cocked to one side,
the little girl's pudgy fingers grasped her grandma's weathered hands,
"Grandma,
your purse is magic, isn't it?"
"Why do you say that?"
The silver haired woman cast a curious gaze on the girl.
The child looked up at her grandmother,
grinning,
missing tooth showing.

"Whatever I need
appears from that bag."
The child's eyes remained fixated
on the black quilted purse.
"What do you mean, dear?"
"Well, whenever we go to the movies
there's always a treat inside."
Grandma chuckled.

Continued

"What else?"
With gentle ease,
the grandmother lifted the girl onto her lap.
"When I'm sad,
you bring out a tissue to dry my tears.
When my lips are dry,
you give me water,
And when I need to talk,
your cell phone is just inside,
and I can call whenever I want
'cause I know you're always there."

The little girl snuggled up to her grandmother.
Grandmother pulled her close.
"So is it, Grandma?"
Is your purse magic?"
The grandmother only smiled
And hugged the child tighter.

29. A HOOKING HUNT

Machrea Kilpatrick, 2011

"IT'S NOT LIKE THE HUNTIN' VIDEOS," Daddy repeated for the zillionth time that night. "There are usually hours in-between deer, and we very well may not see any at all."

I playfully rolled my eyes and picked myself off my parents' bed. Keeping the *North American Whitetail* magazine, I've been reading clenched firmly in my hand, I strode over to my dad's desk where he was zoomed in on the bills.

"I wanna see one like this, Daddy!" I displayed the magazine confidently; its well-worn pages flipped open to a picture of a Boone and Crockett whitetail.

Dad looked up from his work and glanced at the gargantuan buck in the photo. "You've got buck fever bad, girl. That's for sure." He gave me his grin of pride, a look of love that branded me and my siblings as his. It boosted my excitement, and I flung myself back on their bed to pepper him with more questions. Never has an 8-year-old girl been more excited about her first deer hunt.

The next morning, I laboriously waded through my schoolwork, question by question, page by page, minute by minute. Each second seemed to last an eternity as I kept envisioning gleaming antlers in the sunlight, glimpses of darting brown bodies, and the deep earthy smell of resting nature. Finally, after hours of torture, Daddy pulled into the drive. Popping out of my seat, every fiber in my body released like a suppressed spring, I zipped to his bedroom to get dressed. With Daddy's coaching and Mama's oversight, I eventually got everything on. I was wearing Daddy's hunting clothes "because you can't smell like a human." (His concern). And I had a bunch of layers to keep me warm. "Cause honey, you're gonna get cold!" (Mama's concern). Needless to say, I could barely move, but as we climbed into the truck, I didn't really care. My stomach felt like a butterfly hive, and I was rattling off repetitious questions.

Throughout it all, Daddy was extremely soft-hearted to my exhilaration but was continually reminding me that "we aren't going to see anything." I think now, looking back on it, he was thinking, "This girl ain't gonna shut up long enough to see anything!" But that look of pride was still evident on his bearded face when we got out of the car and climbed that huge hill that led to the stand. We treaded up the steep incline, the pine trees above us swaying elegantly in the breeze. I tried to match Daddy's stride step for step, watching the pine needles crushed under his boot shift back into place. The fall beneath picked up the pine needle scent and the dry, smoky incense of shriveling leaves and sent it swirling about us. I was already loving the hunt.

We left the graceful evergreens and stepped out into the power line, the buzzing electrical lines swooping down toward the thick, green grass and climbing back to the next tower. Walking in a mesmerized trance and watching the fizzling lines. I almost smacked into Dad as he abruptly stopped. He turned around and quieted me, motioning for me to stoop down. I obediently hunched over and tried to ignore my instantly throbbing heart and focus on his urgent whisper.

"There's some deer over there!" My pulsating heart leaped into my throat. Wrestling it down, I whispered, "Where, Daddy? I don't see them!"

Stealthily sneaking up the rise, Daddy tried to point out the deer. As I crested the Ridge, I finally saw them, two doe's grazing serenely about seventy-five yards down the hill, completely oblivious to us until I moved. They both jerked their heads to attention and before I could blink, they were bounding towards the tree line, their tails bouncing and abrupt astonishment. I smiled.

"Hey Daddy," I gazed triumphantly into his eyes. "We just saw deer!"

He grinned at me and shook his head. "Just to warn you, honey, we probably won't see anymore."

Stubbornly refusing to allow his bombardment of "realism" to penetrate my exhilaration, I urged him on. Eventually, he got to our tree stand and climbed up onto it. Before Daddy even had all of our gear arranged, I was begging to blow the grunt call, something that always brought in the "big boys" on the videos.

"You really shouldn't blow the grunt call till after the words have settled down," Daddy patiently explained. "Hear how quiet everything is? After a while, all the animals will forget we're here and start running around again. *Then* you can blow the grunt call."

I sighed and slumped on the hard bench to wait. Thirty seconds later, I was begging to use it again.

"Please, Daddy?" I whispered, putting all the 8-year-old cuteness I possessed into the plea. He chuckled at my pitifulness and just shook his head.

I continued to pester him, however, until he reluctantly relented about fifteen minutes later. "But you're not going to call anything in, Hun. it doesn't always work like the movies." He warned me. "And besides the bucks don't come to that call this time of year," he added.

My anxious hands reached out to grasp the call, and I tried to recall the crash course he had given me the night before. Putting every thought into it, I reservedly blew the tubular device. I bent it, fanned my hand over the end, and operated it like a pro. After a bit, Daddy motioned that it had been long enough, so I lowered the call. Instantly, Daddy grabbed my arm and motioned up the hillside. I slowly turned around, and as I did, I heard what sounded like a freight train barreling full bore in our direction. Straining to catch a glimpse of the deer through the remaining vibrant trees, I could see that it was a huge eight-point, his antlers glistening just as I had fantasized while doing my schoolwork that morning. He boldly charged archery and stormed up within thirty yards. Then he harnessed his free-spirited charge and started inquisitively moseying around, his interest piqued but his audacity was gone.

It was then that I got my first taste of that addicting adrenaline. Any hunter knows what I'm talking about. The shortness and deafeningly loudness of breath. The racing heart crowds my Adam's apple. The unsteady, shaking hands. I focused on the deer, trying to keep sight of him through the thicket he was standing in. I could feel Daddy's tenseness at my side; his body was quaking as well. His eyes were probing for a shot through the interweaving branches just as mine were. Thirty seconds that lasted an hour went by. Thirty more. Still, no shot. Eventually, the hefty buck lost his enthusiasm and started to wander off.

I just grinned at Daddy; an unspoken look that was shared that communicated volumes. The excitement, the love, the teasing, the slight disappointment, the importance of the moment, all was covered in that gaze. And I realized I was hooked. Not just on hunting, but on spending time with my daddy, this wonderful man who I am privileged to call my father.

30. LEARNING NOT TO WAIT
Katerina Virostko, 2011

THE IRRITATING BUZZ OF MY ALARM breaks through my dream, shattering a twisted and surreal landscape into a few dozen fragmented images that I won't recall by lunchtime today. I rise from my mattress, slow and creaky as a marionette with tangled strings. Outside my bedroom, there is just a little of the pale, grainy light of six in the morning showing through the trees in my backyard.

It is 6:47 on April the fifteenth when the last vestiges of childhood's sweet ignorance are ripped away. I am in my kitchen hallway, leaning against the fingerprint-smudged wall to tie my shoes and think of the day ahead. *I have, let's see…a history quiz…and a line check…oh, and that worksheet for Spanish. I have to ask Mrs. Cox about-*

"Kate?"

My mother's voice cuts into my litany of things to do before I can leave school this afternoon. It's more than a little irritating, and besides, six-forty-seven in the morning is far too early to even be alive, let alone hold a conversation. It shows in my voice.

"What? We're going to be late *again*, and I won't have time to get to my locker before the bell."

"Grandma Joyce died last night."

She stands there, in the same scrubs she came home from work in yesterday afternoon, like she's waiting for something to happen. Whatever she's expecting, it's not a daughter who sinks all the way to the dusty floor. The sobs are dragged up from somewhere deep inside me, wheezing out like the painful notes of a poorly tuned organ. All I can do is shake. Thinking is completely beyond me. She is taken aback, almost frightened.

"I-I'm sorry. I thought you knew..."

As we rode to school, I sat in the front seat of our van, leaning against the smeary glass of the window and watching the trees and houses and people pass in and out of the range of the van's headlights, fading forever into early morning darkness. It's funny- in novels, all bad news is a punch to the stomach, hard and strong, but it always fades into nothing more than an emotional bruise by the end of the story. Right now, my insides feel like some sadist has scooped out everything with a rusty spoon, leaving nothing but pain and the memory of having had something there, something that belonged to and would always stay. I think I'll always feel this way. Before this morning, death was a kitten who was there in the morning and just gone the next, ducklings who just couldn't make it outside of the incubator, a row of popsicle stick crosses covered with a child's scrawl in Magic Marker that faded in the rain and slowly fell down into the rest of the flower bed. It was nothing permanent, nothing that couldn't be defeated with a deft replacement.

I had always thought there would be more time. She was stable in the nursing home, would probably be there for a few more years. I would just *know* when it was time to go and say goodbye. I didn't have to go in there to see the shriveled, angry husk of the woman who taught me Chaucer and nursery rhymes in French. Surely, she would resurface in time to say goodbye to Kate, not to swear at someone named Margaret.

I was wrong.

I drift through another Thursday at school, an automaton who softly cries in the back of the classroom. By two-nineteen that afternoon, I was all out of teats, and I had come to a conclusion. There will never be as much time as I think there is. I refuse to wait until it's too late again.

Hands shaking, I pick up the handset off the phone. My voice cracks as a voice cuts off the droning buzz of the dial tone.

"Dad? It's me…"

This is the day I learned not to wait.

31. MEMORIES
Meredith Evans, 2011

RUNNING MY FINGERTIPS over the smooth, soft surface polished to a bright sheen, I inhale the sweet, luxurious, yet indescribable scent. What is it? Leather, in particular, my mother's old English jumping saddle.

As a youngster, I was infatuated with horses and everything about them. For what seemed like an eternity, the closest I came to horses was through the vast quantity of equine-related novels I read. I was an insatiable bookworm when it came to horses. I check every *Saddle Club*, *Black Stallion*, and *Thoroughbred* book out of the library. One day while scrounging around in the basement, my sister and I found our mother's tack box, and, consequently, her jumping saddle. Mom had been an equestrian and horse owner before she married my father. McKayla and I immediately begged to buy a bar of glycerin saddle soap like the ones we added to the innumerable lists of horse equipment we had composed while pouring over equine supply catalogs in preparation for owning our own horses someday.

We polished the saddle for hours upon hours. The rich aroma of freshly cleaned leather entranced us as we dreamed wistfully of jumping boldly over fences and returning to a cozy barn to care for our fine steeds. Needless to say, the saddle found a place of honor in our room.

After a considerable quantity of wheedling, McKayla and I were allowed to take riding lessons. I lived for the times we rode. Those days were absolutely marvelous! Not only could I finally ride but lovingly brush and tack my patient equine educator. While McKayla rode, I wandered the barn, standing on my tiptoe to admire the noble Friesians who quietly munched timothy hay in their stalls. I crooned to them as they watched me from under heavy black forelocks. Obligingly, one would leave his fodder and saunter to the edge of his stall and press against the wire to receive caresses on his velvety muzzle. Riding lessons temporarily satiated my horse-crazy longings, but I now knew the realistic ride of riding and horse keeping. I clamored incessantly for an equine to call my own.

One summer I leased Duke, a portly, ambivalent Appaloosa pony. I struggled that summer to saddle Duke myself, I could barely lift the hefty Western saddle onto his back or tighten the cinch enough to prevent the saddle from slipping around his bulging belly. Yet, Duke and I had fun trotting around and around in the dusty arena. I lost my temper and regretted it. I fell off and learned. In the fall, Duke's owner put him up for sale and, after an unfortunate accident at a horse show, it was decided Duke was to be mine no longer.

How my horse-lessness was to be remedied I had not the slightest clue- until Christmas morning when McKayla and I tore wrapping paper off of a box of catalogs, barn catalogs. We thanked our parents, a bit confused as to why they had given us this. Mom explained that she and Dad had relented; we could finally have our own horses in our own barn in our own backyard. We were ecstatic! My father selected a contractor, and we planned the horse "facility." The facility consisted of two stalls, a small pasture, and a little arena. Dad included his horse-loving daughters into the planning, asking us what size the stalls should be, whether we wanted the stalls open to the outdoors and if woven wire fence was acceptable. It was the most fantastic winter spent studying stable designs in *Horse Illustrated* and *Horsekeeping on Small Acreage*.

Later the same winter, I became the proud owner of "Intuitively Obvious," a sweet and sassy thirteen-year-old sorrel Quarter Horse mare, nicknamed "Chloe." While the barn was constructed, I coddled Chloe, brushing her until she glowed. The following summer, Chloe made her debut at Skyview Farm, as McKayla and I called our minute equine establishment. The scent of leather was ever present as I slipped a brand-new leather halter on my equine friend and charge, in celebration of her long-awaited homecoming.

Five years after my dream came true, Chloe and I are still enjoying ourselves, and occasionally, putting our wills against each other. I realize, although I yearned for a horse for years before my mother and father permitted their daughter's dream to become a reality, I learned the value of persistence. My quest for an equine was relentless. A paramount priority in the quest was furthering my knowledge about horses. I devoured tons on every subject to prove my equine fetish wasn't a fleeting fancy. Even when my pleas were met with a deaf ear, I ceaselessly continued to hope while I polished my mother's saddle.

The unforgettable aroma of leather holds many memories and dreams. I will always love the luxurious scent of leather and the feel of a soft, smooth saddle under my fingertips.

32. MAKING DECISIONS
Aaron Laube, 2012

A FEW MONTHS AGO, an ethical dilemma struck me in church. I was reared Roman Catholic, but I have always been more of a moral dilettante, wandering onto the berm of the straight and narrow to pick up the ideas that were dropped by my family, friends, and anyone else I encounter. As a result, I own a mottled, but fairly complete, religious picture. On this particular Sunday, our priest said something in his homily that I had never considered. I understood it, and for the most part, agreed, but I was unsure if it would be compatible with my current priorities. In between homework and a few chapters of *Lord of the Rings,* I mulled over the problem for the rest of the day. I found nothing.

Stumped, I started flipping through my cell phone, hoping it could help me find an answer. Hrunting, as I call him, is rarely as useful as he is touted, but on this occasion he delivered. We eventually settled on three of my friends: Caleb, Caylee, and Alaina. I put my question to each separately. Surprisingly, all three replied. All are intelligent people whose judgment I trust, but from varying backgrounds and with different ideas about religion and about life in general; between them, I'd cover the spectrum as well as the diversity of my 'high council; of friends allowed. My reasoning was that if the three of them agreed on a solution to my dilemma, they were probably right.

I asked them if the new idea and moral goals I was trying to merge were compatible. Caleb and I had a long conversation that basically ended in a resounding maybe. Caylee gave me a "Yes, definitely," and Alaina a, "No. You can do it if it makes you feel better and there might be some good in it." Hardly unanimous. Still, hope remained for my miniature quest. For what feels like a long while I've believed that the correct answer lies somewhere between the two mistakes. I learned that from experience. For much of my life, I've been on one extreme of some issue, and if I hadn't been on the other at some point, I knew someone else who was. In all instances, it wasn't working out for either of us. Even if none of my friends' answers really told me what I needed to know, there might be something of value to draw from their synthesis. Caylee definitely thought there was something to the idea. Alaina had allowed for the possibility of some good from it but insisted that it would not further the priorities that I expressed. Reflecting on Caleb's advice during our conversation in light of the other's responses, I found new relevance in it. The new idea was very tenable; I had simply put it with the wrong objective. What Caleb told me filled the gap Alaina described, and the new idea now served another purpose. The process of solving my dilemma also reaffirmed my faith in this method of making decisions about what direction to advance as a human being. Hrunting, for all his faults, has been rewarded and the will of the high council has come to pass.

33. DEMON DROP: A RIDE TO REMEMBER

Anne Coen, 2012

WALKING IN THE LINE TO The Demon Drop was like walking through a thickening, snake infested mud pit; each step was more difficult and horrifying than the last. I clung to Mommy's hand as a magnet would to metal, silently pleading that the ominous raincloud overhead would drain itself onto the park and we'd have to leave before it was our turn to board. I had no such luck. The gate opened and I followed Daddy and Mommy to our seats, not daring to release my grip on her hand. I cursed her for tying my hair in a high ponytail that morning; if it hadn't been so high, I wouldn't have passed the height restriction, and I'd only passed the age limit by three months. My near ineligibility to ride this coaster made me even more afraid and doubtful of the safety of this sinister, black, dragon. An usher helped me into my seat; it was too tall, and I could not climb into it on my own. He asked how old I was, and I answered him honestly, hoping that maybe he'd tell me I was too young. My hopes were dashed when he proceeded to lock my restraint down to the seat. I tested it to see if it would loosen, or come unlocked, but it didn't. That was it, it was final; I could not escape it now. My tummy became an ocean then; waves crashed inside of me, roaring against their walls. My throat swelled and my breath staggered, struggling to escape my lungs.

I glanced over at my sister to see if she felt as terrified as I did. She was smiling and skittish, rapidly tapping her feet against the foothold. Her face was lit by a mischievous grin; she seemed to crave the thrill of this monstrous ride. She was three years older than I and had ridden many roller coasters before, this was my first. I looked pasted her at daddy, who was relaxed against the seat, a small grin set above his chin, waiting patiently to be taken up. Unable to find reassurance from them I turned to mommy, she noticed my stare and looked down at me. For a moment, I thought she might share my dread, but once again, my hope was severed when she smiled and asked if I was excited. I gulped, and turned away, peering out into the crowd.

They stared at us, waiting to see if we would rise up onto the crest of the coaster. I didn't like the expectant looks on their faces and quickly directed my attention to the passengers ahead of us. Only two more rows had not yet been secured. I watched the usher lock them in one by one, all the while my fear intensified. Shots of panic emanated from the pit of my gut and ran through to my fingertips.

I felt a cold sensation numb my whole body as the last person was latched into his seat. I watched the usher nod to the operator, who then pulled a large, orange lever down, and then there was that awful sound of the brakes being released. My heart throbbed in my chest, beating so profoundly that it must have challenged the boundaries of my small body. Every beat brought me closer to the drop point. My hands became cold and clammy, the pit in my stomach dropped, and I breathed more rapidly. We reached the top and paused.

We were above the noise of the crowd and all of the passengers were silent. The only noises I heard were the ticking of my tinker bell watch and the pounding of my heartbeat.

Tick, ba-bum, tick, ba-bum, tick.

After the third, impossibly long second, there was another sound; a short, gruesome click. Then we were falling.

I opened my mouth to scream but found I had no voice to let out. That sunken pit of my tummy instantly leapt up to my throat and seemed to dissolve, reappearing in its trench to rise up again. The wind thrashed at my face and my legs, unable to reach the foothold, surged straight out in front of me. The clashing screams of my fellow passengers melted into a singular, conflicting shrill. I shut my eyes against the blur of colors in front of me and felt as through I'd be crushed by the force of the fall.

Then it was over. The coaster gently lolled to a stop. The screams were silenced, my stomach was still, and my legs fell back against the seat. We glided backward to the waiting line and the restraints were lifted. Daddy picked me up out of my seat and took my hand to guide me away from the Demon Drop. My legs felt weird as we walked away. I wondered if that was how spaghetti must feel. My mind didn't process anything but that until we were in the streets of the park again. Daddy was kneeling in front of me, telling me I was okay. I felt something cold running down my cheeks and when I wiped it away, I realized I'd been crying. Then I started to laugh and said, "Let's do that again!"

34. FREEZE

Megan Bell, 2012

The wind blows and snow sprinkles the ground,
My fingers freeze and I shiver
Nothing stops me from ringing my bell.

The crowded sidewalk races on
To stores and sales for Christmas,
But many seem to be missing the spirit altogether.

I watch people struggle with their bags
Full of boxes to wrap under the tree,
And faces that look distressed pass by without a thought.

A few pause and look at me
As they wait for the cars to scatter,
Then quickly venture into the sea of mindlessness.

Ding! I continue to make my call
And invite people to share.
For that is what makes the season so cheerful.

Continued

I fade and become invisible
As they shout their plans to each other.
"Two more stops for today",
"A present to buy down the street",
Without realizing I exist.

"Come back!" yells a mother
To the child approaching my side,
And from her raveled red mitten appears
A copper coin.

It is not shiny or new like the gifts from the mall
But a true gift, encircled with love and a smile.

When the penny hit the bottom
Of my rusty, old bucket,
Though small and tarnished too,
For an instant in time, the city did freeze
As they heard the loud clang of that coin!

35. ON THE BACK OF MY HORSE
Grace Parker , 2013

EVERYONE HAS A PLACE they can go to get away from the troubles of life. For some it may be taking a walk through a thick pine forest. The crunching of the dead needles under their feet, and the sweet smell of pine almost seems to melt away all their worries. For others it may be retreating to their room alone and pulling out a sketchpad. With each scratch of granite on paper, they can create a new world on their own to escape to. For me, however, that place of safety, peace, and comfort, is on the back of my horse. Straddled upon her back, I can go anywhere and be anything.

My horse is reddish-brown, like a heartwood of a cherry tree. She is a bay; her cherry-brown coat melts away on her legs and a glistening coal black replaces it. Her lower legs are each covered with a white sock, as if she had stepped into a bucket of white paint with each leg. The sun spills off of her shining coat and makes her gleam like polished brass. She stands out against the thick green foliage of her pasture, like a bright crimson apple against the green of the tree's leaves.

As I walk up to her, she lifts her large head, pricks up her ears, and widens her nostrils to take in my familiar scent. I lean forward, bringing my face closer to hers, and in response she stretches out her neck and touches my small, pale lips with her big, black velvety muzzle. This is our way of saying hello. Next, I put on her bridle. As I slip the bit into her mouth, it clinks against her front set of teeth. I poke her ears through the browband and fasten the silver buckle under her throat. Her big brown doe eyes tell me that she is ready for some fun, and so am I. I gather up the braided, black, nylon reins and swing up onto her broad back.

At last, I'm free. I close my eyes and soak in my immediate surroundings. Her silky coat under my legs feels like a kitten brushing up against me. Her back sways to and fro as she stomps at a pesky horsefly buzzing about. I breathe in the sweet smell of horse, a fragrance that nothing in the world compares to. I lick my top lip and taste the beads of salty sweat that have accumulated on my face under the hot sun. My meditation is abruptly interrupted, as I am jolted backwards with her sudden forward motion. I may enjoy sitting still and enjoying the moment, but my horse, however, does not.

We set off from the ancient, two-story, wooden barn and into her enormous 20-acre pasture at a walk. There is an old wire and wood fence to my right that surrounds her pasture. Some of the posts are weakened from mold, or the years of donkeys, horses, and cows scratching themselves against the rough wood, leaving traces of their manes and tails caught in the barbed wire. We turn slightly to the left, passing a small herd of donkeys, flicking their tails at bothersome flies, and tearing sweet shoots of green grass from the soil. Making our way down to the end of the pasture at a trot we come upon a huge, rusty, red oil tank that still sits there after being retired from use years ago. I tightened my fingers around the reins and signaled for her to go right. A rickety, multicolored truck rumbles by on the road that borders the pasture. The driver and I exchange a friendly wave, and my horse snorts a startled greeting. Turning sharply to the left, we face a towering mountain of a hill. My horse speeds up in excitement, for she knows this is when she gets to run. I smile, lean forward, and drop the reins to her neck. We're gone.

Chunks of sticky earth fly from her hooves as she gallops up the hill. I twist my fingers tighter into her black mane and squeeze my legs into her sides to hold on. The ground is a green blur as I look down over her shoulder. I can feel my horse's movement under me, her muscles tense and relax with the rhythm of her stride. All other noise is blocked out by the hammering of her hooves, and the snorting of her breath, as she sucks air into her lungs in spurts. I close my eyes now, as I flow with her to the beat of her run, a song that we sing together. I feel as if I am part of her. I can fly, so swiftly and gracefully. I am no longer chained to the drudgeries of life, at least not now, during these few moments that I spend on the back of my horse.

36. A RACE FOR LEGS

Harley Hamilton, 2013

WHEN LOVE TURNS TO PRIDE, disaster may strike, as was the case of Dahy the lizard. Dahy loved the races. The feel of dirt under his feet and the air rushing past him as he sped ahead of his adversary gave him a surge of joy. He was the quickest in his animal village and loved by all. Dahy praised the god of speed for giving him his gift of speed and his respect of the races. Yet, the life in his village did not satisfy him, for he desired to race others who were swift footed like himself. So Dahy left his beloved village to race in other nations and even in the Great Games held annually for legged animal competitors.

As Dahy began racing he began to get a reputation as the unbeatable racer. Lemuel, the cheetah, was deeply devastated when he lost to this quick lizard, for he was known as the fastest of all animals. However, being the good sportsman he was, he congratulated Dahy and told him, "Dahy, the god of speed, Omnipotent must have gifted you deeply for you are the fastest animal I've ever raced." Once Dahy might have thanked Lemuel, but Dahy's love for the races had become tainted by his growing arrogance from winning all of his races. His love for the race had become a love for winning. Dahy haughtily exclaimed, "That old god has not gifted me with any kind of gift! How could he when I could beat him at a race myself!" The cheetah sadly shook his head at Dahy and departed after saying, "My poor friend, your ignorance will be your downfall."

The god of speed, Omnipotent, heard what Dahy had said and grew furious for he had indeed gifted Dahy more so than any other animal before him. Omnipotent decided to test Dahy and give him a chance to redeem himself before omnipotent punished him. Taking the form of a lion, omnipotent went to the earth plane to race against Dahy. Dahy was already on a racing field when omnipotent approached him. Immediately, Dahy was challenged to race which he quickly accepted, still gloating over the fact that he had outrun the cheetah. Dahy sped into the lead right away leaving his opponent behind. He was unaware of the fact that the lion was deliberately losing. After the race, omnipotent gave his congratulations to Dahy, and, like the cheetah, he told him he must have been greatly gifted by the god omnipotent. Dahy grew angry and once again claimed to be better than the god of speed. Furious, Omnipotent changed back to his original form and commanded Dahy race him. Dahy, frightened by the might of the god, obeyed. Like before Dahy took the lead quickly and didn't see the god for most of the race and thought, "Ha! I was right! This old god isn't faster than me!" Omnipotent was still at the starting line, letting Dahy grow in confidence. As Dahy neared the end of the race Omnipotent began to run. Much faster than Dahy, he soared to the finish in seconds. When Dahy finished the race, amazed at the speed of the god, he received his punishment. Omnipotent, God of speed took Dahy's legs, preventing Dahy from ever participating in his beloved races ever again, as he became the first snake in existence.

37. FINDING WALDORF
Megan Van Horn, 2013

HE RUSHES INTO PLACE, skidding to a stop behind a fishmonger's stall. Brushing wind-blown spices from his shirt, Waldorf adjusts his ubiquitous glasses, preparing for the inevitable. He affects a glassy stare, gazing into the hazy barrier that separates the reader from the chaotic, scrambled-egg mess of characters. Waldorf catches brief glimpses of the child behind the nebulous obstruction, that dastardly fourth wall. She appears rather old to be reading a child's book, her dark hair skimming the pages, precipitating ripples in the ether as her dragonfly eyes flicker from person to person. A long oval appears in the distance, racing closer and closer toward his position behind the rather odiferous tuna.

Zing. The pad of her finger brushes against a tangible surface. And Waldorf feel it, Thurm, through his inked bones. Every time he is found, it touches his poly-paper heart. The purveyors of the ethnic stands in the world marker of this page pause in their bustling, all sounds ceasing as they jealously observe his feet lift ever so slightly off the ground. The clarity in his glasses sharpens into focus, and, for one brilliant moment, he feels like he touched the sun as he sees her quietly satisfied face. Then, the flash is gone, the colors dim ever so slightly, and the weight of gravity forces its way back onto his striped shoulders.

Page twenty-four darkens. As soon as he's sure that he's out of sight, Waldorf races stage left to the trapdoor he was shown when the original Waldo of this book planned an extended vacation to the emerald city in the Wizard of Oz, Waldorf being the understudy, naturally. Normally, on his dashes through the under-world tunnels, Waldorf occupies his time thinking about the creature comfort of his small apartment on page eighteen, above his Julia's florist shop, and how much he'd dearly love to be there, in his favorite armchair. Getting stroked by a sticky fingerprint generally wasn't his idea of congenial time, and that, unfortunately, occurred more often than he'd prefer. But, this time, he was instead imagining the life of the reader above him. Right at that moment.

Popping out of the paradoxical cool, yet flaming oven, Waldorf jostles the muffins the baker holds as he extracts himself from the brick passageway. The stripes on his shirt snag on rough edges, and, not for the first time, Waldorf feels a bit a fool, tugging at his loose ends. He straightens. The girl looks to be having a spot of difficulty on this go-round, and it takes all Waldorf has not to jump and wave his arms. He knows. He perceives her sense of wandering, the hesitation marking the path of her fingers as she journeys across the paper above. Instead of her touch caressing him, he wants to comfort her and tell her that, though things seem unclear and vague right now, though she knows not who she is and where she will end, she will always be found by the right people. *Zing*.

38. WE WERE STUBBLE SOLDIERS: A CUTTING-EDGE WAR TALE

Becky Downing, 2014

THE TIME HAD COME. After many days of procrastination, I finally came face to face with my fate. I had known that this would be needed for quite some time; the show choir Christmas performance for a nearby nursing home had been written on my calendar for weeks. My short, crimson, Amish-looking dress hung beside me. A symbol foreshadowing what would meet me tomorrow. Inspiration for what I needed to do now. I slid my hand along my leg. It was time.

The battle would be fought in the deadly waters. Boiling hot steam danced atop the surface as if Beowulf's serpents were preparing to blow fire from deep below. I stepped in, afraid Grendel's mother might lunge at my feet, provoking me into a duel, but I was here to fight another battle.

My "sword" glistened in the corner of my eye. I had heard legends of this dastardly weapon. Greek mythology states that it was created among the valleys of the planet Venus. Its sleek design and sharp blades intrigued philosophers far and wide until one day rumors of its existence reached King Gillette's ears. Nestled on the fiery volcanic tops of a Venusian Mountain range, King Gillette's castle became the destination of the philosopher Nair, who brought forth the weapon to the king. Angry with what was before him, the king ordered Nair to put the weapon on the next chariot to Earth. Thus, from the valley of Venus, the banished weapon ended up in our convenience stores.

I grasped this cosmic tool as I slid it across my flesh. Each sharp blade came face to face with the stubble soldiers on my leg. The commandos clenched to their spots, holding on for dear life, as each blade advanced on like cavalry of English fighters. It wasn't long until the cavalry wiped out every soldier in sight, leaving nothing behind but smooth terrain. But wait!

As my eyes scanned the war zone, I noticed the remnants of a bloody trooper left behind in battle. The gliding weapon had done its job, but one brave soul must have fought back valiantly, resulting in an all-out duel between stubble and blade. The latter left with a victory, but the soldier ended up leaving gory traces of his doom atop the smooth battleground.

I tended to this area, cleaning up the remnants of war with a hot rag. As I wiped up the guts and gore of the soldier, I couldn't help but think of the life It left behind. He had a wife. A family. And I had separated him from it.

Still, duty calls. And when the sounds of Christmas carols fill up the distant skies, there is nothing that can stop me and my blade from wiping out the stubble soldiers' camp. When the nursing home calls for holiday cheer, we ride.

39. ROOTS AND BEANS
Sarah Holdren, 2014

"TALL WHITE CHOCOLATE MOCHA," I anxiously tell the Barista, forgetting my manners for the time being and rudely shoving my card in her direction. The details of my transaction a blur, I stroll over to a corner where two chairs await and plop my flustered frame into one, attempting to hide my stress in the wrinkles of the plush leather.

A few minutes pass and I hear the familiar string of words that often inhabit my coffee runs, yet this time the words do not contain the same comfort that they usually do. "White mocha for Sarah," a man calls from behind the counter. I slowly stand and saunter over to claim my usual drink, pretending to forget my uneasiness.

I struggle to undo a perforated cardboard sleeve to slide around my scalding coffee and hear the chime of the bell at the door, signaling the entrance of a new customer. I look up and suddenly the cacophonic noises of the café fade into the distance, now only a muddy blend of laptop keys and muffled laughter. It's her.

A tall, thin woman, only slightly more aged than my grown siblings, enters, tosses her thick brown hair out of her face, and adjusts to her surroundings. She looks around as if she is searching for a familiar, yet unrecognizable face. Finally, as if God had forcibly moved her line of vision, himself, she sets her deep blue eyes upon me. Greeting each other without a word, my inhibitions fade with an innate recognition that this is good. Feeling the years of separation slowly evaporating like the steam off my hot coffee, I embrace my birth mother for the first time.

The next few hours are a blur. She orders her usual drink, the same as mine, and then continues to prompt me about my life. I tell her about my childhood, laughing at how easily the memories come flooding back to me in her presence. My illogical fear of grass. My brother's cruel, but somehow hilarious teasing. My uncontrollably bossy ambition. Every seemingly unimportant aspect of my childhood, every little worry about momentous accomplishment, now seems like the most pressing issue of her life. With her blue eyes glowing and her wavy brown hair bouncing with every giggle, I begin to trust her. Slowly, I open up.

My questions are endless. "What about my dad?" "What do you do?" "Do you have a family?" "How do you get your hair to look that way? Mine always looks like Hagrid!" Her answers are as expected. My dad left her a few years after my parents adopted me. She works as a nurse in Columbus but wishes she had gone back to school to become a doctor. I do have some siblings, but they are unaware of my existence, and she wants it to stay that way. As for her hair, she uses some sort of homemade relaxer. Although simple, the answers do fill a void. They are the roots to my tree- the genesis of my identity.

An espresso machine squeals a high-pitched scream in the background, letting off its steam and drawing me back to reality. I wake up, startled to find myself back in my sunlit room. The familiar smell of generic coffee and homemade pastries filters up from the kitchen downstairs. "Sarah, breakfast is ready!" my dad calls. I drag myself out of bed and stumble downstairs to where my loving parents are waiting for me. "No white chocolate mocha with a side of fantasy for me today," I think. For now, she can remain in the subconscious of my dreams. For now, I do not need her to be a reality.

40. NIGHT TERRORS
Olivia Holbert, 2015

WHEN I WAS YOUNG, I was afraid of the dark. As I grew, I learned to cope with the absence of light, because darkness was not frightening in itself. Instead, I came to fear the things that seethed in the void. Shadows were living nightmares popped from the deepest recesses of my mind and splayed in corners too shaded to see clearly. Dimly outlined shapes were gruesome, twisted figures that could only move when I wasn't looking. Rustles of movement were the claws by which the terrifying creatures plaguing my thoughts tore through the carpet toward my paralyzed body.

My own imagination filled the night with terrors beyond my control, and I never thought it could be any worse than that until my imagination locked on something infinitely more probable: *death*.

I reached a point when I was no longer afraid of the dark, or even the monsters that occupied it.

I was afraid of dying.

The Angel Azrael appeared in my dreams and enclosed me in his midnight wings. The silken feathers filled my lungs and extinguished my screams; I dissolved until I was just another part of the darkness. The hounds of hell bade up my window and scratched at my door. The sound of their snuffling held me suspended in a lucid state where I could neither move nor speak. They lurked in packs at the edge of the yard, their bodies made of thick slabs of shadow and decay. I feared the time they would raise their muzzles to the moon and howl for my capture, The Grim

Reaper himself, grasping the pendulum that marked the end of my days, gestured from the end of my bed and held the folds of his ink black cloak aloft. Inside, tortured faces swarmed and swirled in the awaiting void.

I was an inconsolable wreck. How can one escape the evil manifestations of one's own mind? I closed my eyes, I blinked, and I saw the twisted, rotting visage of my own corpse. I considered each breath my last. If I ever found myself in a quiet, solitary moment, then a palpable terror seized up my throat and weighed heavily in the pit of my chest.

I resigned myself to a state of constant unease. I would just have to learn to live with this debilitating anxiety. I would have to learn to live feeling half crushed beneath my own sense of dread.

Until, finally, the day came when -nearly unremarkably- that apprehension thawed.

It began with a conversation about star-crossed lovers.

"Romeo and Juliet are great and all until you realize they're totally just insufferable kids that want to rebel against their parents and end up killing themselves in an attempt to prove that their love was real," my friend had complained. "You want to talk star-crossed lovers? The sun and the moon are the real great star-crossed lovers of this world, not some dramatic 14-year-olds."

I thought it was a bit foolish to assign such an innately human emotion to inanimate objects, but I figured the point was less about love and more about the "star-crossed" part.

"No way," another friend had insisted. "The sun and the moon have nothing on the supreme polar opposites of Life and Death."

"How so?" I asked, with an eyebrow raised and a suddenly sick feeling pooling in my gut. The mere mention reduced me to quivering.

"Assume that in some version of reality apart from our own, Life and Death are sentient beings," she began. "One cannot exist without the other, but their very natures repel. The only time they ever touch is a split second—a mere infinitesimal fraction of a moment—when a living creature dies. Yet no matter how much time passes, Life continues to offer its creations to Death, so that even for the briefest instant, they brush fingers. That's love."

I'm not scared to die anymore.

I am Life's gift to Death, and I know that whenever the time may come, Death will take good care of me.

41. HEAD ON
William Lekan, 2015

WE MET OUR ALASKAN ATV GUIDE, a white-haired man with playful eyes named Heiny, at a grocery store in Wasilla an hour or two prior to the dreadful ordeal. While on our two weeks summer vacation in Alaska, my mom's motto was "ADVENTURE", and on her master's list of adventures, she included ATV riding, since none of us had done it before. After careful perusal of entries written on *Yelp.com*, she and her boyfriend came to the conclusion that Heiny's services were the most impeccable, trustworthy, and professional in the apparently extensive business of Alaskan ATV expeditions.

While we waited in line for the sandwiches we ordered, he shared with us an elaborate anecdote of the time he heard a caribou fart. This should have been an immediate red flag to us. His valued customers, who placed, to some degree, their lives and their hands, but we just laughed with some unease, then got our sandwiches and left, heading for the campground where we were to meet him.

We engaged in a limited discourse with Heiny, as we adjusted our helmets and gloves, climbed into the seats of the ATVs for the first time, and figured out, between us, the location of the transmission and brakes in an attempt to get at least a vague idea of how our foreign vessels operated.

After Heiny had dressed in gloves and a helmet, he gave us a rambling instructional lecture on the ATV, including, as if it were an afterthought, some advice about rocks ("Take them head on. Follow me, and don't try to drive around.")

Keep in mind, dear reader, that nothing was mentioned of a river. Nothing was mentioned of the Himalaya boulders that would block the road, or of bears, although spending a single day in Alaska was enough to make this threat abundantly clear. Heiny toted a gun around on his belt, which he patted smugly at various moments during his speech, his gentle way of reminding us that all animals were fated to die by his hand.

Driving down the initial stretch of paved road, my confidence about the trip ahead was high. I was, perhaps, even enjoying the experience. I felt it akin to barreling down in a giant, overpowered golf cart. Then, at what seemed like the peak of my joy, we pulled over. Heiny, planting his feet on the ground, turned to look at me with a smiling face and hollered, "Give it some more juice! Don't let these *girls* get ahead of you."

He was talking about my mom and little sister, who rode behind me on the same ATV, my sister in the back because my mom feared she wouldn't be able to handle driving on her own. In truth, she was the most adventurous member of our family, constantly reminding us of her plans to go skydiving in New Zealand when she turned 16.

We started to drive again. I squeezed the handlebars with angry fists, a minor effort to win back my masculinity.

Heiny jolted to a stop and made a sharp right. We were guided down a narrower path made of dirt, pine trees looming over us, and behind them, the mountains watched like stoic sentinels.

There was a distant noise, the unmistakable rush of water. We halted for a few dreadful moments as Heiny listened with a puzzled expression as if calculating something in his head.

"We might be able to go across," he said after a while. Across? The *river?* I hoped I misheard him. We curved around a patch of trees. The sound grew louder and more powerful until it was deafening.

Then it materialized before us a thick dark current, wild and threatening. I glanced up and down for any side of a bridge or a way around I might have missed. Nothing.

"Wait here," said Heiny.

He proceeded to drive forward into the water. Smoke rose from beneath his ATV, seeming to threaten imminent destruction. But then, miraculously, he was parked on the other side, smiling and waving A welcoming hand, a signal that it was okay to follow him. None of us moved.

"Just follow my path!" He called. It took me a few moments to realize it was my turn. I pretended to mess around with some imaginary gauge on the handlebar, so it looked like I was just checking the air pressure or something, a normal preparation for my descent into the river.

I heard a faint echo of Heiny's taunt, whispering through the breeze: *Don't let those girls get ahead of you.* I was a man. I could handle this. I lurched forward into the river.

My ATV resisted, like a dog pulling on a leash, and emitted a series of horrible gurgling noises. At that moment, any manliness I pretended to possess had drained. This was the end. I was going to die.

I stopped halfway across. Whether it was by conscious choice or if I physically wasn't capable of gaining speed any longer, I don't know but I felt that as long as I sat there, nothing terrible could befall me. It was certainly safer than the alternative, which was to try driving forward, end up getting pulled down the river, falling off the ATV, and drowning.

Over the rush of the current, I was dimly aware of Heiny waving his arms and yelling vague instructions like, "Keep going!" and "Into the current!" But none of them registered. I couldn't move. My whole body was frozen.

When he came to the conclusion that no amount of yelling was going to alter my repose, Henry stepped into the river. He was knee-deep in water by the time he reached me. "Get in the back," he said. I obeyed.

As we drove back to shore, I felt the sting of failure. I hadn't made it across. This naturally felt like the climactic moment of the trip I thought that, and the normal course of events, everything following it would make me feel like a denouement. Unfortunately, real life wasn't a three-act plot structure, and the perils grew more and more daunting. For one thing, the paved roads became noticeably absent and were replaced by the most rock-intensive trails I've ever seen.

At one point, one of my tires managed to get lodged between two rocks, and if I hadn't shifted my weight in time, I easily could have flipped. Henry's only advice consistently seemed to be to not slow down and to "drive through the rocks," as if driving through rocks were something that people were naturally inclined to do. He told us offhandedly about a woman who flipped on a previous expedition. "She was fine!" he assured us.

I eventually realized that Heiny's advice was harsh because it was utterly unembellished. It was dry, direct, and to the point. This wasn't necessarily a bad thing, I was afraid to drive over the rocks, so he told me. I should have been motivated to try harder, but instead, I found myself wondering how anyone could possibly think this activity was enjoyable, rather than finding joy in it myself.

By the end, we were all exhausted, and when we finally took our helmets off, I felt simultaneously relieved and glad to still be breathing. Later, as I lay in bed that night, I would still feel like I was being jolted from side to side, and I would hear the vibrating din of some hallucinatory motor. For weeks to come, I would harbor resentment towards any river and or body of water. I would shudder at the smallest bump in the road as I drove down the Interstate. ATV riding was a powerful experience, an experience that I would endlessly struggle to erase from my memory. Although being distant enough from it has made me glad to have had it. Experiences like these, I've found – turbulent, wild, and unforgettable – are the best kind.

42. CONFESSIONS OF A COMING-OF-AGE LIAR
Madeline Barry, 2016

THE FILM ADAPTATION OF *The Perks of Being a Wallflower* hit theaters my freshman year of high school and created one of the most unnecessary frights in my life. The *Perks* novel has been considered one of the most accurate and heartfelt portrayals of teenage life ever to hit the shelves, and the movie was equally as good. Everyone loved it, everyone wanted to see it, and "everyone" included all the people I had known in middle school. All the friends and classmates who had tuned into my brief but thrilling friendship with Brandon Hayes, the cousin of my neighbors who came to town every few years for extended stays.

Brandon has two sisters, Grace and Marie, who we would babysit quite often when his mother decided to meet up with other friends and family members in the area. He and I had the same taste in film (something I take *very* seriously), the same dorky sense of humor, and a love of late-night conversations. He and I would wander the town for hours, finding or creating mediocre adventures that would make fun memories for later and befriending anyone we encountered. These moderately interesting stories came up at lunch and study hall in school whenever Brandon came to town. He and I were as close as two people could be, but there's a catch: Brandon wasn't real.

Brandon was a figment of this creative outsider who wanted to test out her story-telling and character-creating abilities. For a while, these stories harmed no one. I got to practice my comedic chops and entertain everyone around me, and no one had any reason to question the authenticity of my romps. Until the day someone asked what he looked like. That was pretty easy to gloss over— "Oh, he has dark hair and brown eyes, you know?"—and everything went back to normal. A few weeks later, someone asked for a picture. That was a little more challenging, but I made it work. At that point, I was going through a bit of a Logan Lerman phase, an actor a few years older than I who had been making films since he was three. If he was in it, I had seen it. None of the friends with whom I shared these stories spent a great deal of time watching TV, let alone researching their favorite actors, so I felt pretty confident when I marched in the next day with a picture of Logan Lerman from his early teen years. Those who wanted to put a face to the stories had their wish, no one questioned the shots of the boy I presented, and life continued on. Brandon faded from my stories, having finally decided that this fictional creation had had a good fictional life in my stories, and I sent him back to his home state and out of my stories.

The Perks of Being a Wallflower was released barely eight months later, and I began to realize my predicament. I read *Perks* in my early middle school days, and I was in love with the story from the moment I started it. When the trailer was released, I insisted on having my closet friends gathered around me for its unveiling. I realized my error in mere moments. The trailer opens with the lead character narrating his goals for high school over a montage of his post-eighth grade summer. The lead character's name is Charlie. In the film adaptation, Charlie is played by none other than Logan Lerman. I thought I was dead. I thought I would surely be found out.

If anyone found out I was lying, the image of the eccentric and likable, Maddy Barry, would surely fade into oblivion as the Maddy Barry who spent most of her afternoons watching the news and biking to the local CVS to buy anything on sale would come into the spotlight. I never created these stories to hurt anyone or make anyone feel bad, but rather to find a sort of acceptance I had lacked in my earlier years of school. Not only did my classmates eagerly listen to my quirky adventures, but this person I had created, Brandon Hayes, accepted me too. As a figment of my imagination, I could choose whatever path I wanted him to take, including the route of thinking Maddy Barry was genuinely cool, despite her over exaggerated stories and lack of any fashion sense whatsoever. If anyone knew he was fake, I'd have to acknowledge his lack of existing as well, and fourteen-year-old Maddy Barry, who played clarinet in the marching band and was second string on the JV soccer team, couldn't stand the thought of rejection in that instant.

I felt the blood drain from my face as the trailer continued on. One hundred and forty-six of the most anxiety inducing seconds this teenager has ever had the misfortune of living. As the trailer ended, I slowly shut the computer, waiting for a response. Six of my closest friends were circled around me in that moment, six opportunities for my very delicate world to crumble into a mess of self-loathing and humiliation.

"I can't wait to see that!"

"Me too!"

"Let's all go together!"

The chipper voices of my friends rang out in lighthearted enthusiasm, eventually closing the mental void I had created in self-defense. I heard myself say, "I can't wait to see it either." No one noticed the gaping hole in the stories of a fictional friend, and if anyone did notice, they were kind enough to let me continue down my rocky path of self-discovery. I did see the movie. I loved the movie. I didn't see it with my friends though. I saw it with my parents on my birthday and watched the physical manifestation I had assigned to my brilliant and accepting creation portray the completely and unquestionably fictional character to Charlie.

The Maddy Barry who is finally putting this experience into words no longer needs to create people to satisfy a need for acceptance, though she is not above the occasional exaggeration for the sake of a good story.

And, if my dear friend Brandon Hayes could catch a glimpse of the person he's helped form today, I hope he would see how his existence, be it for the sake of my story telling or desire for approval, has helped me step toward a greater form of being. One person I made up on a snowy weekend in January in 2011 has impacted me more than an imaginary friend should impact a teenager. But, despite the fact that lying probably isn't the best way to come of age, I wouldn't change a thing about the fictional boy who allowed me to also create the version of myself I didn't even realize I wanted to become.

43. EMPTY OCEANS
Jacob Bird, 2016

Waves will form,
In a cylinder of ink.
They carry a great weight,
Shatter this ship.

Oh, mourn the sea foam.
Where'd my color go?
Black are the floods,
That move out,
And in.
Of the metal,
Jagged tip.

Here comes the dead.
Floating in the deep,
Bellies swollen with hate.
Lethal marks of ink,
Brought them to their knees.
Shouting at the hull.
Bracing for the black tide.

The ocean,
Then sang.
She brought forth the cold,
That washed them away.
But now she's all alone.
There are no sailors left.

44. MORNINGS
Kylie Dougherty, 2016

I remember all the mornings
the coolness of the air in the summer
the warmth of multiple layers in the winter
calves going baaa saying "I'm hungry"
the once fresh air filled with manure
setting up milkers
getting cows in
the scream of the motor
the process begins
wipe, wash, wipe
put the milkers on and wait
the cow kicking teat dip
the bitterness as it enters my mouth
repeating the process over 100 more times
It will never end
cleaning the milkers when all the cows are through
the hiss of the air brakes as the milk truck backs in
the sun climbing over the hill
the meow of the cats as they get fed
the weary walk up the hill with milk
it feels like a mountain
the calves need fed
the swish swash of water
as everything is cleaned
my morning is over
my day is just about to begin

45. BLLLAAAARRPPP. BLARP. BLARP.
Alayna Cowden, 2017

IT'S ME. IT'S ME. They can all hear it. Of course, I am the bone-head that thinks she can get away with just a tiny rubber stopper to keep her cello from sliding all over the glossy wooden stage floor at the State Orchestra contest. And here I am, struggling to keep the stupid thing standing, sending fart noises into a dark, echoing, abyss of an auditorium.

Not only am I experiencing the malfunction of all malfunctions, but I'm sitting first chair. First. Chair. Front and center. Everyone in the first row is looking at me with one of those annoyed expressions that say, "You about done messing around?" Everyone not in the first row (and there-fore much less serious about it all to begin with) is stifling giggles. My director is raising her eyebrows while trying to keep her own professional composure.

I can hear the announcer reciting the rules of the contest, and I know I'm running out of time. But the cello still won't stick! I try licking the bottom of the rubber stopper, and that doesn't work, and sure does taste awful. I even tried taking off the stopper and wedging the metal tip of the end pin into a miniscule crack in the hardwood floor. Failure again. I try placing and replacing it, saying a prayer, licking it, spitting on it, blowing on it, and anything and everything else I can try. I feel like giving up. Just as the announcer says his last words, I take my shoe off and use it as a stopper for the end pin. It looks crude, but it works.

Despite my success, I can't trust my size 8 black ballet flat to pull through, so I spend the entire performance gingerly playing and squeezing the cello with my knees to hold it up. We make it through the final song and relief cascades through my body (and now my aching knees) now that I no longer have to fret about my farting cello.

The following Monday in class, we listened to the judges' recorded comments on our performance. And of course, at the beginning of every recording, are the distant blaaarrpps of my farting cello, a humiliating reminder of the vast difference between music and noise.

46. BASSOON

Bennett Van Horn, 2017

Obscure and vivacious, I am
At once both a doddering grandfather tromping along
And a chorus of geese.
I am the post of a bed
And yet the hidden gem of the orchestra.
Both mocked and revered am I,
Sought for and despised.
Being the butt of jokes
Gives me quite the personality.
Force life into me
Through my
Narrow
Neck
And I might sing.
I both stand alone and support my fellows.
A duality of wood and nickel.

47. THE PERFECT POOLSIDE PARTY
Brittany Smith, 2017

IMAGINE AN AFTERNOON in the late July heat. The warmth of the sun radiating off of everything it touches. Consider the backyard of a rural home perfectly planted outside of town. A large, blue pool with crystal clear water is the center of attraction; but there is a nicely shaded deck complete with a patio table and chairs surrounding it. Today was the first day in the week that the rain had stopped, and the sun was glowing. Little did I know today was meant to be a blessing in disguise.

The door of my home bursts open with such force that I know automatically who is about to walk in. A very petite woman runs through the door and exclaims. "It's party time!" Today is a combined birthday party for my sister and cousin. The woman is wearing her favorite summer tank top and jean shorts that give her little body some shape. Her expression and mood does not hint at the evil in disease that is raging on inside of her, but her skin is very pale, and she is as skinny as a rail. These are effects of the disease, and they show how much her body is betraying her. The one thing that always sticks out though is her eyes. They are like the ocean, or at least what it looks in pictures, and they show all the excitement that is to come.

The person to whom she is speaking is none other than me. I am 14 and she is 35. She is my aunt, and we have always had a unique relationship. I have spent hours upon hours with her since I was a baby. Our bond has been untouchable since the moment I was brought into this world.

We basically have become each other's best friend. She has called me Britty for well, as long as I can remember. Her kids have mostly known me by this nickname, and it is a creative name I have grown to love.

"I believe you know what time it is," my aunt says as she lays down all the ingredients, she brought so that we can cook.

"I always know that we have to cook as soon as you barge through the door," I reply with excitement etched across my face.

"Come on, it's time to get the oven heated up and crank up the music!"

I turn on our favorite songs and we grab the recipes we need. All the pans clank together and cause a huge ruckus as I pull them out of the cupboard. Shortly after we've found all the utensils, bowls, and ingredients we need for the food, my kitchen fills with the symphonic sounds of cooking. Together we accomplish most of the cooking and go outside to cool off in the pool with the rest of the family. The water is so refreshing to cannonball into.

A couple of hours later, the grill is fired up and the air is filled with the aroma of the traditional cook-out food (hamburgers and hotdogs) we always have. A time after that, everyone files out of the pool and dries off with huge beach towels. We all go inside and grab a paper plate that seems to have an insufficient amount of room considering all the food we have laid out. All my aunt says is, "Dig in, enjoy, and one plate is NOT enough."

When the time comes, I clamber up the stairs and yell as loud as I can, "PRESENT TIME!" My sister and my cousin bolt down the stairs. The family gathers around the birthday girls as they tear into their beautifully wrapped gifts. Their screams of excitement and pure joy fill everyone with happiness.

Once present time draws to a close, everyone disperses to different areas of the house. My mom suggested that my aunt watch a video called *Twerk Intervention* on her Nook and that was when the real fun began. My aunt sits down on the table and then as the video progresses, she jumps out of her chair and says, "Britty look I can twerk just like this girl." She says this as she tries but fails to twerk.

"You're going to hurt yourself if you try any harder," I tell her as I try to contain my laughter.

"I'm doing it right and nobody can stop this crazy train from dancing," my aunt says as she continues to struggle.

The video ends and nobody can stop laughing. Luckily, she stops just as my grandparents pull up in the driveway. They would not have thought her dancing was as amusing as the rest of us did. We all greet them on the deck, and we sit around the patio table in the shade. We discuss various topics before my grandparents leave.

After a long and exhausting day, we all say our goodbyes and express how much fun we had. We hoped to see the whole family again very soon. Everyone had even started planning a party for next year. My aunt leaned in before she left and whispered, "I love you to the moon and back and we will go homecoming dress shopping alone together very soon."

This is our last time together.

The next week, the illness takes over her body and she is sicker than ever before. She sleeps a lot and does not really talk to anyone. It was the inevitable end everyone had dreaded for so long.

I wake to the sounds of my cousins playing at my house on August third, and I know something is wrong. My mom merely confirms my worst fear, taking away an irreplaceable piece of myself. That is why every day when I look out my window, I hope to see two butterflies flying around wildly without a care in the world. This I know is a sign from heaven saying, "I'm here, no matter what the distance."

48. FETIAL

Sarah Vejsicky, 2018

The enemy ambushed us.
A spear was tossed into the soil,
Forgetting I was in the way, and now I was a diplomat, one who shot
Barrages of feathers in place of powder.
I was now a liaison who tried reason
But, no, that wasn't in their
Rules of war, how inconsiderate was I?
How dare I send doves in place of pigeons,
Olives instead of lychee,
People instead of men?
The energy called for an armistice,
Sending quills, asking for what I could give as
Penance for what I had done-
What had I done? The spear stayed despite this
Cloud of unknowing.

The enemy ambushed us.
They spat a torrent of words on the ground,
Forgetting I was in the way.
Now I was a civilian, one who tried
To fight with distance in place of territory.
Then a victim, I fought
Slander, that vicious, vindictive beast
Which latched onto my shoulders and
Weighed anchor before my navy was ready.
They wrote over my rules of war in red,
Vengeful corrections were made in favor of low-lying
Trenches. Be careful; they grab your souls there.

Continued

The general demanded I be submissive for what I had done.
For what I had done? The spear stayed despite this
Change of attack, even though my eyes saw
straight through the fog of their defensive line.

I ambushed the enemy.
I scattered a handful of modest words,
Ignoring who was in the way, and
Now I was the ruler, the one who
Abandoned the fight in favor of her own riches.
The enemy was now powerless. I fought
Slander, I cast off reason, all in favor of my
Rules of engagement, new edicts written in black and white,
An absence of gray- that was a rebellious flag.
I built mountains over trenches; their glorious
War machines cannot reach my city in the sky.
I demanded nothing for what they had done-
What had they done?
The divot of the spear remained
Despite this treaty, which my eyes saw as only
A brief end to what had just begun.
So let us go to war on my terms.

A note to my reader: "According to book one of Livy's History of Rome, after Rome had been injured by another state, four fetials were sent out to seek redress. One member of the verbenarius carried herbs gathered from the Arx on the Capitoline Hill. Another member called the pater patratus, served as the group's representative. Upon reaching the border of the offending state, the pater patratus first announced his mission and addressed a prayer to Jupiter in which he affirmed the justness of his errand. Crossing the border, he repeated the same form several times. If, after 30 days (some sources give 33), no signification was given, the pater patratus harshly denounced the offending state and returned to Rome, where he reported to the Senate, if Rome decided to wage war, the pater patratus returned to the border, pronounced a declaration of war, and hurled across the boundary either a regular sphere or a special stake sharpened and hardened in the fire, this ritual was supposed to keep Rome from waging an unjust or aggressive war. If, however, the hostile country was far away, the sphere soon came to be cast upon a piece of land in front of the Temple of Bellona in Rome; by legal friction, that land was treated as belonging to the enemy. Thus, the ritual limitations were overcome by such legal fiction, in the state entered into any wars that were seen to be its advantage."

"Fetial." Encyclopedia Britannica, 25 Feb. 2016. www.britannaica.com/topic. Fetial. 31 Jan. 2018

49. MILKSHAKES, FRENCH FRIES, AND EVERYTHING IN BETWEEN
Emily Dietz, 2018

THOUGH THE SUN had long ago slipped out of view from the diner windows, the old man remained in the corner booth, sipping decaffeinated coffee.

• • •

A boy with wide eyes and hand-me-down clothes, he had begged his mother to sit at the counter the afternoon he drank his first milkshake. He ordered chocolate, at his older brother's recommendation, and when it arrived his mother insisted upon taking a photograph. He posed, grinning widely enough to expose his missing front tooth, but was laughing at something his father said when the camera finally flashed.

The other front tooth was lost eating french fries with his brother and grandmother at the table against the back wall. His parents were bringing his new baby sister home from the hospital, and in his excitement to finally meet her, he left the tooth lying on the diner table, forgotten. When he realized what he had done, he burst into tears, but his mother reassured him that the Tooth Fairy would understand and even appreciate his desire to spend time with his sister.

After his brother's fifth grade baseball team won their tournament, he and his sister got to tag along to the celebration. They sat at the end of one of the long tables, giggling happily as if they were a part of some great secret. The coach brought a cake from the bakery in town, chocolate with buttercream frosting his favorite. As he ate, he dreamed of being an athlete just like his big brother and of having a party just like this one thrown for him someday. And soon enough, he was in high school and on the football team, carpooling with his teammates and sitting in the same booth every Friday before the game. They would order something new each week, competing to see who would try the most ridiculous thing, and talk about the latest high school gossip until they almost missed the bus. They kept the tradition alive outside of football season too, bringing notes to copy and flashcards to study.

The diner was one of his favorite places to do schoolwork even without his friends, and he made a habit of drinking coffee at the table in the comer with his books spread out in front of him. So, when his shy, brunette history partner asked where he wanted to meet to discuss their project, it was the logical place to bring her. They worked at a table near the center of the room something new each week, competing to see who would try the most ridiculous thing, and talk about the latest high school gossip until they almost missed the bus. They kept the tradition alive outside of football season too, bringing notes to copy and flashcards to study.

She made his life impossibly bright, whether it was helping him comfort his sister after her most recent break-up, drinking milkshakes late at night with their friends, or just sitting at a table for two, staring into her sparkling blue eyes, and talking about the future. But all too soon, the future became the present and summer morning breakfasts turned into going-away dinners. He was headed across the country to join the Air Force; she was attending college and working in a bookstore. They said goodbye at the table where they'd first sat, both promising to write, but leaving it at that.

They did write at first, but were quickly swept up in new, separate lives. The letters, once full of promises and declarations of love, became less and less intimate until they stopped coming altogether. The years passed; he traveled the world, met new people, and experienced new things until his childhood was all but forgotten. But when he ended up back at the diner, sitting by the window on a bleak and cloudy Tuesday, all of his misplaced memories came flooding back. It was crowded that afternoon, with passersby ducking in to escape the rain, and he was busy reminiscing, so when she walked in, he almost didn't notice. She walked hesitantly over to his table, hiding behind her hair the way she had in high school, and asked if she could sit. He nodded, and it was almost as if they picked right up where they'd left off. She'd changed, of course, they both had, but somehow, they still fit together as well as they had in high school.

She had become a schoolteacher, and just like before they would meet at the table in the middle of the room after school. They were married in the summer, surrounded by family and friends, and it seemed right that the reception dinner be held at the diner, where they'd shared so much of their lives. The night ended happily, with tears of joy, lots of laughter, and love.

But not all their moments together were so carefree. Money was tight and arguments frequent, and although the good times outnumbered the bad, he often found himself grabbing two chocolate milkshakes as a peace offering. Before he knew it, two had turned into three, then four, and he was bringing his own children to the counter, cracking jokes like his own father while his wife snapped pictures.

The kids' school years flew by, and they too went off in separate directions, visiting on weekends and holidays, full of stories about life on their own. He worried constantly for them, but was mostly proud. And soon he was happily retired with his loving wife, passing the time by starting projects around the house, traveling to places they'd always talked about visiting, and relaxing together. As she aged, he took care of her every need, provided for her every wish, and thanked God for all the memories he had been blessed to share with her over the years.

After she passed away, he visited his children and grandchildren more often, making new memories. He spent more time with his siblings and old friends. He enjoyed sitting in the diner and watching others: families, groups of teenagers, couples young and old. He even learned to laugh again, although his life was never quite the same.

• • •

As it neared midnight, the old man finished his coffee, slowly rose from his booth, and walked through the diner's glass double doors.

50. LONELINESS

Hannah Stoepfel, 2018

Loneliness sucker punches,
Catch me unaware.
My friends, a threesome,
Sashay ahead whilst giggling
And murmuring secrets,
Oblivious to me;
Not deliberately,
Surely,
But nonetheless,
A pang of longing sears through my chest.
A sigh escapes, noiseless:
A silent lamentation.
One that, sadly, typically,
Remains unanswered.
Approaching the steps, now a whisper behind them,
I listen to the cacophony of my emotions
Rather than the gossip.
I linger at the top of the stairs,
Determined not to grieve through the remainder of the day.
Artificial smile in place, I continue,
Pretending as though things are perfect.
Like I always do.

51. TRI-VALLEY "ICE" SCHOOL
Alyssa Shawyer, 2018

ON A SCORCHING DAY in August, I observe hundreds of students slowly walking into Tri Valley High School. As they walked through the doors, The sudden temperature change from the summer heat to the bitter chill of the air conditioning shocks them. A few of them are grateful for their relief from the heat, but many instantly began rubbing their arms to maintain their body temperature. And seeing this would bring a huge smile to my face, if I had one, for my plan is prevailing.

The kids sit in a small, dark math classroom trying to focus on the lesson, but the Arctic temperatures distract them from their work. They ask the teacher if she could turn off the air. Reluctantly, she walks over to me, flips up my protective cover and presses my up button to raise the temperature. I chuckled to myself because I know her efforts are in vain. I work to keep the building so frigid that I can hear the sound of the students' teeth clicking together as they chatter during a cold chill. No matter how hard the teachers try, they cannot fix me.

When the class is dismissed, I can hear the students talking about why the school is so cold. I'm amused by the creative answers I hear: One girl who was dressed in long pants, a T-shirt, A sweatshirt, and a thick blanket draped around her suggests that the administration does it so that they will be discouraged from breaking the dress code. Another thinks it's so that the stinky students won't sweat or smell as bad as normal. Still another thinks it is a tactic they use to keep students awake, and the district has so much money that it just wastes it on excess air conditioning. The true reason for the low temperatures is that three years ago, maintenance turned me down extremely low for a record-breaking hot day and I got stuck right at that temperature! No one has been able to fix it since. Luckily, I happen to love being extremely cold and at a steady temperature all of the time.

The students walk into the huge cafeteria. I can tell they expect it to be warmer. All of the warm, crowded bodies should keep it nice and toasty; However, that is not the case. It is the coldest room of all! I watch as the kids race for the tables lining the outside of the room closest to the windows, hoping that a little bit of the warmth from the sun will reach them. Among the roar of the voices, I hear the tapping feet, constantly moving and trying to stay warm. Many of them are complaining about being cold, and a petition has even started to raise the temperature of the building.

I am frightened. I've been at the same temperature for three years, and it has been the best three years of my life. I hate being bossed around and changed all of the time. Teachers walking up to me every period, wanting it two degrees warmer or two degrees colder. I thoroughly enjoy staying right at the same temperature and not having to adjust to new temperatures and situations every half an hour.

On the next day of school, all of the students walk in wearing winter parkas and boots despite the 95-degree temperatures outside. After I watch all of them file in, I noticed something odd. I see the maintenance truck pull up to the building. Two men get out holding toolboxes. This is the moment I've been dreading. I'm finally going to be fixed. The men walk up to me and remove my cover from the wall, exposing my internal wiring system. I feel slight discomfort as they poke and prod at my wires. Finally, they step back, and I feel my temperature rising. I hear the students erupt with cheers and applause, and I realized maybe being warm isn't so bad.

52. BOYS WILL BE BOYS
Katie Frame, 2018

A TWELVE-YEAR-OLD GIRL walks into her sixth-grade science classroom and sits at her desk. Her notebook is out, her pens and highlighters are ready to go, and she is ready to learn about her favorite subject. Her dream is to be in the science field, perhaps an engineer or physicist. Flashforward six years and that same girl is walking across the stage to take her diploma. It is announced she will be going to a small private college to major in English. She has forgotten about her sixth-grade dreams of being in the science field, but why? Throughout her childhood she was constantly belittled. Adults told her the science field was not one for a woman, and women definitely did not become engineers or physicists. Science was not girly, she was told. She was told to lean towards something she would have a better chance of getting a job in as a woman, such as a teacher, nurse, or journalist. Her lab partner in her senior year Advanced Placement chemistry class, however, was going to the Massachusetts Institute of Technology as a chemistry major, with hopes to be a chemist. This boy was never belittled or steered towards different careers. The boy's love of science was encouraged throughout his childhood, and it was never an embarrassment for him. He was allowed to be in the science field because he was a male, and males dominated the science field. This is male privilege. Male privilege is more opportunities for better careers, better pay, and better choices. Male privilege has opened the door for females to lose control of their own place in society, their own bodies, and their own confidence in themselves.

Think about the options of majors for high school graduates. Doctor, biologist, teacher, real estate agent, veterinarian, or interior designer. Without realizing, one typically will assign a gender to fit the role of each of these careers. Doctors are usually male because men and women are told to be nurses. Biologists, or any type of scientist, are also male dominated. Teachers, real estate agents, and veterinarians are more inclusive. Male teachers are not uncommon, and female veterinarians are not uncommon. Why have these careers been assigned a gender? Why do some careers not have a gender? At what point did we as a society declare that being a teacher or a nurse is a better job for a female than being a brain surgeon or an aerospace engineer? At what point was it declared fit for a male to be the sex that should know how to drive a manual or change a tire? Why should women not know how to do these basic tasks?

It is because at some point in time, women were delicate creatures. Men were the dominant sex, and women were told to stay at home. Once women began gaining rights, they began finding jobs. These jobs were seamstresses, teachers, or maids. This was hundreds of years ago and yet the tradition has stuck. Women trying to breach the medical field are often belittled and scoffed at. Women trying to be attorneys are stereotyped and considered to be the bossy female, but when men become attorneys, they are better when they are commanding. This is male privilege.

Women have been taught to sit down and be quiet. From an early age, girls are picked on and made fun of by boys on the playground. They are shoved, hit, and mocked, but they are told they cannot do anything about it. Why not? Well, because boys will be boys. They are told the boy in question just likes them, that is all. Little girls are told to accept their torment from boys. They are told they are overreacting. They are told they cannot defend themselves. They are told it is their fault, not the boy's fault. This is fair? Of course not. However, "boys will be boys" is part of society. Worst of all, it lets boys believe that to show they like a girl, they must make fun of her, push her, and degrade her. Girls are taught this is normal. This is male privilege.

As a young woman, it is hard to build self-confidence. In group work, someone seems to always take charge. Someone has to always be in charge of what the group has to do, who will accomplish what task, and how everything will come together in the end. From a young age, that person is usually not a girl, unless there are no boys in the group. If a girl tries to take charge, she is told she is being too bossy. She is told she is being too commanding. She is told to sit down. She is told her ideas are unimportant. A boy will step up and take charge, demonstrating the same traits the little girl just did, but no one says anything to him. No one says he's being too bossy. No one says he is being too commanding. No one tells him his ideas are unimportant. The group goes along because even as children it is drilled into our heads that men should lead. Men are strong; therefore, they make good leaders. Since men make good leaders, we should wordlessly follow them. This is male privilege.

Girls are taught to protect themselves but not too much. A woman that hits the gym every day and can bench her own body weight is considered too powerful. No, women are taught to defend themselves in a different way. They are taught to carry pepper spray in their purse, and they are taught to carry their keys between their knuckles so they can stab anyone that tries to touch them. Women are taught to always have a trusted male with them walking alone, or if a male friend is not available, to always be on the phone with someone when walking alone. Women are taught to defend themselves against attackers. They are taught to cover up so they will not provoke any wandering eyes to follow them home. Men are free. Men do not have to carry pepper spray or hold their keys in a defensive position. Men are not concerned with being cat-called. Men are no concerned with being raped. Meanwhile, a woman should never walk past a man on a street alone and not on the phone or with her keys in position between her knuckles. This is male privilege.

A woman at her firm could be the most loyal and hardworking employee there. She could have clawed her way up from being an intern. She could get all her work done, reviewed, and published in record time. She could be overly prepared for meetings with papers, statistics, a power point, or even all three. She could be working her hardest because she is dedicated to her job. She could have been there for over ten years. She could notice her boss looking at her a little too long, and the wandering eyes of her male colleagues. She would ignore it because that is what women do. She would think this is normal. She would think back to when she was at recess and her male classmate chased her around the playground as she yelled for him to stop, and the teacher told her that her classmates just liked her, that was all. She was told to ignore him. She was told that boys will be boys.

So, she would ignore her boss's comments and her co-worker's eyes, despite the fact over half of them have an expensive wedding band on their left hand. She would not care. Why should she? She was told at a young age that boys will be boys. She might think it was her fault, that maybe she was not covered up enough. She would remember her college days when her friend was raped, but it was quickly decided it was her friend's fault because her dress was just a little too short. The woman would decide she would cover up more for work. She would not think twice when her boss pulls her into his office and tells her an opportunity for a promotion has opened up. She would know that she deserved it, even though she would never say that her boss watched her every step as she left his office. She would notice when her co-worker got the promotion she deserved because the boss "took a chance" on the new guy. The new guy that was hardly ever prepared for meetings. The new guy that had only been at the firm a few years, compared to her decade. The new guy that stared at her despite the wedding band on his finger and the picture of his two little girls by his computer. This is male privilege.

Male privilege is telling a little girl her dream cannot be reality and telling a little boy never to give up. Male privilege is telling a college student it was her fault she was raped because she was dressed so provocatively it was no surprise her male classmate could not control himself. Male privilege is a hard-working woman who has been at her firm for more than ten years being denied a promotion in favor of her male colleague who takes sick days often, stares at his female co-workers even though a wedding band shines on his left hand and has only been at the firm a couple of years. Male privilege is striking the fear of God into women at a young age about walking alone in the dark. Male privilege is women believing they have no right to certain things, even their own bodies, in the male dominated field.

53. HOTEL WAFFLES
Chad Bell, 2019

One dark and dismal day
In a land far, far away,
I tried to make a waffle
Which turned out truly awful.

I began that fateful morning
With joy and no forewarning;
I thought I could with ease
Make a waffle, "it's a breeze."

"Put the batter in a cup"
So I tried to fill it up.
And what to my dismay
"fill it up just halfway"

No problem said myself,
I'll put it back upon the shelf.
Yet being the go-getter,
I thought some's good, more's better!

I began to pour the mixture
Over top the waffle fixture.
I tried to act with haste
For fear that I would waste.

Pouring done I closed the lid,
But then it o're-flowed the grid!
Squashing out the sides it flew
Down the pan onto my shoe!

Dismayed but not distraught,
"I'll get my toppings now," I thought.
Butter and syrup I spied
Beyond the people, they lied.

Through the crowd, I swerved and ducked,
To the toppings, I then plucked
The condiments that I desired
Deliciousness was then acquired.

Back to my iron, I did go,
But then I shouted, "Oh no!"
Gone too long I didn't turn
The precious waffle that now did burn.

Black and dark it was like night
Everything was not alright!
To the trash, the waffle went
Then its death I did lament.

54. I AM AN AVALANCHE

Austin Parry, 2019

My birth is an act of destruction,
My living, is my dying,
My life, a too thin candle
Bright, energetic, but fleeting.
My power is stored, in layers,
And is set free, in a tear.
As I live, I grow in strength,
Devouring everything in my path:
Deer, trees, rocks, humans.
All meaningful, but it matters not,
For I cannot change, what I eat.
I only live as I can, rushing down,
To my end, my glorious death.

55. AN EXPERIENCE I WILL ALWAYS HOLD CLOSE TO MY HEART

Sierra Chambers, 2019

THIS PAST SUMMER my life changed unexpectedly as I received the opportunity to go on a mission trip to Haiti. It was truly an eye-opening experience that taught me to truly be grateful for everything I have and never take anything for granted. The Haitians barely had anything but were still the happiest people I have ever met. This taught me happiness does not come from material things, rather it comes from your attitude and level of gratitude. We went to change their lives, but they ended up changing our lives as well; it always seems to work like that when I serve others.

A little over two years ago a new pastor who goes by Pastor John joined our small church in East Fultonham, Ohio. Pastor John began sharing stories of his past fourteen mission trips and explaining how we could also make a positive impact in Haiti. It had always been a dream of mine to go on a mission trip, but I had never been out of the country or even on an airplane, therefore I was extremely nervous by this whole idea. Surprisingly, my mom, who had also never been out of the country or on an airplane, began talking about wanting to go on this trip. Pastor John's passion for the Haitian people and my mom's motivation inspired me to overcome my fears and step out of my comfort zone. After a great deal of preparation and the addition of fellow missionaries, the mission trip to Haiti was set for the summer of 2018.

After piecing together our team of twelve people, we realized the group consisted primarily of teachers and youth who had a desire to work with children. Therefore, we planned a Vacation Bible School (VBS) and Teachers Conference for our time in Haiti. We put together five classes for the VBS based on the interests of our team members which included Bible study, music, crafts, hygiene, and sports. I assisted a young adult who recently graduated as a Dental Hygienist in the hygiene class where we taught the children the importance of brushing their teeth and washing their hands. Before and after each day of VBS, we held a music ceremony which included a group of hired Haitian musicians who led the children in songs. Our VBS also helped to temporarily ease one of the children's greatest struggles, the lack of nourishment. During both days of VBS, we provided a meal to the Haitian children which was more than many of them would have eaten in about three days' time.

There were approximately 300 precious children who attended VBS full of energy and vibrant smiles. The language barrier meant nothing to them, and they were overjoyed to be there. During the opening and closing ceremonies, they sang and danced their hearts out with no regard to whom was watching. Their eyes sparkled as we handed them tooth-brushes and toothpaste in our class and three girls washed our hands out of gratitude after we taught them the importance of washing their hands. I also never imagined the joy and excitement a Dum Dum sucker could bring to a child. While we were passing out suckers to the children, the moment the suckers were within arm's reach, it was game on. There were more children surrounding me with outreached hands than I could have ever imagined. My time with the children was priceless and truly made all my stress and worries disappear.

Each class of the Vacation Bible School had translators to facilitate communication with the children, however, within no time the translators became our friends. Jackie is the name of the translator I spent the most time with and he was truly inspiring. He speaks several languages including French Creole, French, English, and he is in the process of learning Spanish. Jackie is currently a teacher at the school we were utilizing for the Vacation Bible School and his goal for the future is to learn as many languages as he can and attend Law School. He practiced his English with me and taught me some French Creole. I learned from him what it is like to be a young adult in Haiti, and I shared with him what it is like to be a young adult in the United States. Through Jackie I learned the importance of seeking knowledge and setting goals. I am thankful for the time I got to spend with Jackie, and I hope to see him soon.

The following day, our teachers met with Haitian teachers for a conference to discuss the similarities and differences between schools in our respective countries. A few Haitian teachers even traveled eight hours by foot and crossed a river in order to attend. The main concerns of our teachers were that the Haitian teachers had little supplies to work with to provide these children an education. It touched the hearts of our teachers and left me with a call for action.

After careful thought and long deliberation, I decided to utilize my role as National Honor Society Vice President to lead and organize a schoolwide collection of school supplies to send to Haiti. Teachers and students alike donated the necessary items which made me feel like the collection brought our school community together as we supported schools outside of our community. After all was said and done, we raised approximately 133 pounds of school supplies which will be greatly appreciated and have a huge impact on Haitian schools, including one preexisting school and one that is soon to be established. They will also allow the Haitian teachers to provide a better education to the students utilizing the school supplies they receive.

The most memorable part of my experience was when Pastor John taught us the valuable lesson espoused by President Ronald Reagan "We can't help everyone... but everyone can help someone." There was a little girl who loved to hold our hands as we walked around the area, and he allowed us to bring her to the house in which we were staying. We truly spoiled her, giving her a coloring book, crayons, a baby doll, snacks, water, and other small items to enjoy. I even had the opportunity to change her into a dress sewn by my grandma and put new shoes on her feet. We spent about an hour loving and spending time with her. This demonstrated to us that even though we personally would never be able to help everyone in Haiti, we had the power to change the lives of the people around us, wherever that may be. I am forever grateful for this experience because it helped shape my dreams and plans for the future. It helped me overcome some of my fears, venture out of my comfort zone, and gain a brand-new perspective. As it turned out, the hardest part of the trip for me was leaving. I grew as an individual in faith and confidence while being surrounded by constant love. I would encourage anyone who receives the opportunity to go on a mission trip to accept the invitation with an open heart. This trip was more valuable to me that any amount of money and I would do it all over again in the blink of an eye. The Haitian people will always hold a special place in my heart, and I cannot wait to go back.

56. THE LITTLE LEAGUE SLAM AT DAIRY DUCHESS
Avery Adams, 2019

IT IS A TUESDAY morning in June, and 1 finally roll out of bed. Still in recovery mode from the long weekend of travel softball, I trudge into the bathroom to get myself refreshed and ready for the day. My plans for this evening involve me doing absolutely nothing. I always try to give myself a day to lay low after playing an insane amount of softball in the draining sun the past several days. As I'm brushing my teeth, I fantasize about the day of relaxation ahead of me, but then it hits me, and I freeze: I have work tonight. Although bummed by the fact that I no longer have the day to myself, the idea of going to work is fortunately not a dreadful experience for me. My Tuesday night adventure at the Dairy Duchess presents me with many fluctuating emotions, demands hard work, and guarantees special memories, especially on Little League night.

The clock ticks closer to three o'clock, so I start preparing for the wild night ahead of me. The lunch I pack has a much higher nutritional value than a meal from "The Duch" would ever provide me. I slip on my super fashion-forward Skechers and throw a hat on. I cannot forget a sweatshirt as although it is the middle of summer, the ice cream shop is still shivering cold. My watch reads 3:25, and I start to panic, I'm going to be late! My idea of late is when I arrive 20 minutes before shift change rather than 25 minutes early. Most of the employees stroll in at 3:59, but that is not how I roll.

As I am on my way to the shop, I think about how the next six hours will unfold. The girls working tonight are all veterans, and our favorite manager is on shift, so it is going to be a fun night. I pull into the parking lot and try my absolute hardest to avoid the ginormous pothole near the entrance, but I fail miserably as I hear and feel the bang of my tires traveling in and out of the crater. I walk into the shop to be greeted by my hilarious, hard-working managers and the day shift girls. Then, I clock in, wash my hands, and stock up the frozen food and all toppings needed to make the night much easier on us.

When I see the girls that are working with me tonight enter, I know shift change is approaching. Our manager splits the tips, and we say goodbye to day shift. The real party happens at night. But before all the excitement, the Dairy Duchess enters into a daily stage that we like to call the calm before the storm. Nobody, and I mean nobody, will stop by for a treat. All you hear in the shop during these phases are the frequent shattering of freshly made ice inside the ice maker and the constant churning of the slushy machine. Although this dead period is extremely boring, we take advantage of the situation by getting the chores that are typically started at closing time finished early in hopes of a premature clock-out time. Sometimes if we have extra free time, we play cards or mix various slushy flavors together in hopes of inventing a new favorite. This luxury doesn't last for long. Out of the corner of my eye, I see a car pull in. "Woohoo! A customer!" we say. Then, I see another car, and then another, and another, and another. They're all minivans. Be careful what you wish for.

The once tranquil ice cream shop turns to complete chaos after the weekly little league baseball games. I hear the crackling of cleats against the pavement and soon see the mad rush of elementary boys yearning for juicy fried food and a creamy milkshake. No place other than the Dairy Duchess have I witnessed such excitement as the boys' cheeks and palms are smashed against the glass window while they impatiently wait in the growing line. The humorous part of this experience is that the dads of the players are just as excited for a treat of their own, while the moms are relieved that dinner is covered for the night. My coworkers and I all look at each other, take a big deep breath, and smile. We are ready for action. My manager takes the orders, while us girls prepare the food and ice cream. The conversations held at the window between my manager and the boys are so comical. Not only are they funny, but I can often predict what kid will order which treat. The little scrawny outfielders make it to the line first, for they are probably the type of kids who yell at their parents when the button to open the sliding door of their Toyota minivan does not open the instant Dad puts the car in park.

My manager Jody always starts the orders by sliding open the glass door and leaning down to reach eye-level of the kids while saying "Hi, how may I help you?" The little speedsters typical responses include "large vanilla cone," or if they are feeling hungry, it is a "hot dog plain, ketchup only." These little brats are never polite and always order the most basic flavors on the menu. Big boy on the other hand, who happens to be next in line, gets a real man's meal from the Dairy Duchess. I am on grill duty for the night, so I am expecting to hear the printing of a long grill ticket. This slugger is most likely a first baseman and is always very respectful. His order usually goes a little something like this: "May I please have a double cheeseburger deluxe, an order of fries with ranch, and a large chocolate cookie dough milkshake?" After he completes his order, he smiles ear to ear and anxiously waits on the bench for his grub. These orders continue for about twenty minutes, and the rush of making numerous snowstorms and bagging up onion chips results in spilled milk everywhere, grease all over our shirts, and cookie dough pieces stuck in the grout of the floor tile.

Finally, the rush is over, and all that is left in the windows of the shop are remnants of fingerprints on the glass. We check the clock and jump with excitement! It is closing time. Our favorite part of the night is when my manager yells "Hit the lights!" and we all race to turn off the beaming open sign to keep annoying customers away. The cleanup process begins now. Nightly chores consist of wiping the machines down, filling up toppings, replacing outside trash, dishes, sweeping, and the one chore that everyone dreads: mopping. No one ever wants to mop. So, guess who always gets stuck doing it? Me. I do not mind, for it only means that the day is coming to a close. When finished, I dump the nasty mop water into the drain and clock out for the night. I chat with my manager in the parking lot before I unlock my car and start it up. Mission complete.

As I make my way home, I reflect on the night and chuckle at all of the incredible moments that took place. I arrive home feeling sore and exhausted, but the tip money was worth it! Although that teeny tiny, monotonous building lacks exterior character, what goes on the inside of the shop has had an incredible impact on my life. As I head up to bed, I feel very thankful for my privilege to work with such great people at my hometown's lone ice cream shop. I am ready for the next shift.

57. TALISMAN
Ava Moore, 2020

IT IS VERY STIFF AND VERY FLAT across the bottom. It definitely doesn't conform to the shape of my head like I hope it will. The fuzzy, brown pipe cleaners stretching from one side of the base to the other act as an anchor to my thick, dark hair. After sliding some brown hair clips underneath the pipe cleaner and snapping it onto my head, I shake my head left to right, up and down. The smooth shapes of my glass rattle in their silver casing, giving off a sound as a jingle bell would, engulfed tightly in a child's palm. With a deep breath and a glance in the mirror, a smile creeps onto my face. I really earned this, I think, as I rotate my head in every direction, assuring that the circular base is lying flat across the top of my head. The four points stand tall, glittering with my every move. My hand reaches up to touch the cool headdress. It is real. The day of earning my title remains unforgotten; the baby of the group succeeding on her first try.

It was blistering hot that day, the sun beating down on the small town of Miamisburg. Girls filed into the Baum Opera House with garment bags in hand, and curlers in hair. I sit in the corner and the bustle of women around me, arranging all accessories and makeup products in performance order. With organization being my nervous habit, no sequin is out of place on competition day. A friendly face smiles and sits at my table, throwing everything in a glittery pile on the chair to my right. We talk and laugh, and I bury my nerves deep in the pit of my stomach; as the youngest of the group by a stretch of three years, I have to hide my intimidation. The combination of nerves and the cool breeze from the air vent above me sends chills down my legs, despite the heat outside. I wrapped my cotton robe around my shivering figure, taking a deep breath, hoping for smooth sailing during a long day of preparation.

As the evening drew to an end, a 10-minute interview was completed, a question on politics was answered on stage, an exhausting dance routine was performed, and a trip (almost turned into a complete fall) occurred in a cheap gown. The oldest woman of the group pats my shoulder as she passes, offering a side smile that says, better luck next time. Taking the millionth deep breath of the day, I lift my chin and enter the stage, following the other women as we prepare to hear the results. My heart races and palms grow clammy. The burning lights hanging from the rafters illuminate the small and crowded stage, with each contestant standing shoulder to shoulder. My feet shake in my 6-inch platform heels as the master of ceremony stands center stage, headdress in hand. I am almost numb as I hear my name echo through the boxy speakers sitting in the two front corners of the stage. I pick my jaw up off the floor and walk center stage, feeling the cool rim placed on my head. Did I really do it, I think, am I really worthy? My smile stretches from ear to ear as I reach my hand up and touch my head as an 18-year-old, standing in front of a 25- year-old, glittering.

58. CHILDHOOD BAKERY

Megan Knicely, 2020

The sun wakes to
two young sisters eagerly
pulling Grandma between them.
They bound over brick road
indulging the playful wind
in their pursuit of the treasured Christmas tradition:
"Cookies!"
They burst through the door to
sweet aromas that enveloped them.
The familiar display of
vibrant treats invites anticipatory grins.
Giggles fill the air as
sisters agreed to share delicacies.

Continued

Two teenage sisters
resurface from an automobile,
approaching the new site. The
foreign building bears
a nostalgic name, but
lacks comfort of memories.
Ponderous doors open on a
corporation where crowded
customers debate selections. The
pungent scent of coffee
capsizes tranquil dreams.
Each sister invests in her

emerging adulthood:
dark, bitter liquid
permeates the membranes
of their tongues.
Fantasies of sugary treats have vanished.

59. DESPERATE
Alexis Salsbury, 2020

You're fifteen and so desperate to be thin
that you miss months' worth of meals.
Your stomach rebels
the growls and sharp pin pricks of hunger grow in fervency each day.
You are resolute, though.
For each cramp of discomfort, you run an extra minute
until you can bring yourself to look in the mirror again.
Food isn't food anymore:
you're down to a few hundred calories a day, but will it be enough?
If you can reach one hundred pounds, will it make you happy?

You're sixteen and a beautiful boy likes you back
You're so desperate to be loved
that you ignore each flashing warning sign, begging you to turn back
on the road to "happiness".
He loves your body, isn't that enough? Isn't that the same thing?
Social media, friends, and co-workers are all monitored.

Your friends call him possessive, but it feels sort of nice to be possessed,
doesn't it?
At least someone cares.
And when that beautiful boy's ugly claws of jealousy sink into you,
you look in his angelic face, his crystalline eyes,
and you tell him he's all you'll ever need.
As the line between love and ownership blurs,
you wonder if his idea of love will finally make you happy.

Continued

You're seventeen and rapidly forgetting what it's like
to feel anything besides empty.
One small, resilient corner of your mind is championing your will to live
while everything else shuts down.
Your world exists in a state of extremes.
There are no in-betweens.
Either you sleep your days away
or you spend each night chasing rest and release from your thoughts.
Eating goes the same,
for you either lack the energy to make even the simplest of meals

or you engorge yourself on any comfort food you can find
in the vain hope that it will fill the void.
Feigning normalcy, you joke and socialize as you once did.
No one seems to notice
as you check out of each conversation you force yourself into,
but you didn't really want them to notice,
did you?
If someone noticed a change, then you'd have to admit there was one
and you are truly—and possibly irreparably—different now.
What will it take for you to be happy?

Continued

You're eighteen now and desperate to not repeat the past.
You can eat what you love without fear
of the supposed damage it may cause.
Your old favorite jeans fit again.
Your mom has finally stopped searching your face
for signs of concealed hunger.
There is another beautiful boy now
who has never asked you to drain yourself

just so you can fill him up.
He holds you close,
and there is safety in the world again.

There are still days when you'd like to stay in bed while life marches
endlessly, tirelessly
on without you.
The war your mind continually rages against you is far from over.
You're getting better at standing your ground, though.
It isn't exactly happy, but it's a hell of a lot better than
hopeless.

60. BEHIND OF THE VEIL OF CRUELTY
Adelaide Pitcock, 2020

Samuel Pisar*
16 August 1943

WITHIN THE CONFINES of the rattling box car, I could smell the paradigm of human atrocity before I even saw the clouds of wispy ash slithering from the towering smokestacks. Auschwitz... a living nightmare... a whispered tale of horror on ghetto street comers and in dim rooms... the place of no return.

After our human stampede stumbled from the rickety, splintering car, we began the ominous march across piercing pebbles and dusty dirt towards the looming guard bouse. We were faded figures, decrepit and fraying, emerging, as if from our own vintage postcards, into the throes of death. As we trudged onwards a rusted, curved sign, "Arbeit Macht Frei" (Work Will Set You Free"), greeted us - a forsaken message, a horrid irony. Suddenly, another faded figure erupted from the haze and bolted toward the green, grassy lands of freedom beyond, his last sound a cry of anguish, rendered silent and helpless by a resounding bang from above.

It is as if we have all become a mass of puppets on makeshift strings, but as we attempt to peer behind the curtain for the source, the puppet master, we discover that the strings never terminate; rather, they stretch interminably towards the sky and disappear into the choking smog.

"You have come to a concentration camp; there is only one way out- the chimney"... the first words I heard here will forever echo as a tormenting chant inside my brain, a dreadful warning... We have entered the dungeons of hell, where hope is a mere memory.

Half of our group has been sentenced to a line threading away from the barracks, plodding onwards toward the portentous chambers of smoke. I can see their puppet strings catch and pull; they are condemned to a rapid blaze that spins out of control, leaving behind only a trial of ash...

Vinzent Klose**
16 August 1943

EVERY DAY I AWAKE to the same smell of wretchedness, the putrid odor of blazing corpses, the odor of death. It seems that my vision and so many others' are clouded by the haze of cruelty. I toil for the inhumanity of man within this barbed-wire fence, planted by the seeds of loathing and the capitulation to evil, and I, too, play a role in this villainy...

A new mass of ragged, hopeless met a catered these confines today, and I felt like a puppet in a larger game as 1 sorted them into lines, half condemned to the gas chambers, half seemingly redeemed ...my pointed finger became the wire of a pendulum, swinging towards life and death.

Later, as I lingered outside the door to the chamber of no return, where innocence would soon be annihilated, I felt that pendulum crash and burn amongst the thousands of prisoners I have sentenced to the chambers of death. I gave the silent order to begin the gassing, and the screams of the prisoners within hell's pandemonium commenced. As I stood in the blanket of darkness outside the crematorium walls and watched the gaseous remains float towards the heavens, I began to fear that the power of this malevolence is insurmountable, and we will forever be haunted and ravaged by its aftermath.

Samuel Pisar*
9 September 1943

HERE WE ARE STRIPPED of the right to live and behave like normal humans; we have become skeletons of men. Even the inhumane vastness of this camp cannot contain the depth and magnitude of the unfathomable deeds carried out here. This morning the same wagon that delivered our measly rations, meager portions not even fit for a rat, was laden with the bodies of the thirty-one dead from my barracks. Later they were shoveled into a mass grave like a heap of forgotten rag dolls.

I have come to realize that the world's cruelty is inescapable, lurking in every corner—in the faces of the guards, void of emotion as they aim their metal barrels at a line of cowering men and in the vindictive faces of degraded, desperate prisoners who nick scraps of food from their neighbors. But most of all, this cruelty manifests itself in the deep pools of despair reflected in our eyes and is tattooed in five numbers carved in purple ink on our forearms.

Vinzent Klose*
9 September 1943

ON RAINY DAYS my boots sink deep into charcoal-colored dirt and muck; on clear ones, my skin prunes under the mid-afternoon blaze, and my drab green uniform, a costume of monstrosity, sticks to my body.

"Bereite deine waffen vor!"

Seconds after the order arose, twelve guns, including my own, clicked to the ready. I peered down its barrel to the line of cowering prisoners, resigned to their fate, doomed for stealing scraps of food from the morning wagon.

Did they know that as the sun rose in the sickly yellow sky this morning, it would be their last day to view the heavens above and breathe this filth-infested air?

Another order arose to fire in "Drei..Zwei…Einer…"

The manipulative marionette strings of devilry have bound another victim yet again... Eleven other guns erupted with rapid fire as I watched in trepidation as men fell like dominoes, and my finger shook and wavered around the trigger…

---

*Jewish lawyer and writer (March 18, 1929 -July 27, 2015), Survivor of Auschwitz. His parents and younger sister Frieda were killed during the war. Transferred to Dachau concentration camp. Escaped during a death march.

** SS commandant at Auschwitz, Guard Battalion NCO, SS-Oberscharführer

61. IN REVERENCE OF MY HERO

Cambria Beane, 2020

Red, white and blue
Stars and stripes pulsing;
Under my hand
My heart overwhelms me with pride.
Explosions of sound yield
Images of my grandfather's stories

Crossing the vast blue sea
Vietnam:
Endless green and heroic helicopters.
I see the red, burning flames
As he crashes into a mountain.
I have seen this cane transform into a wheelchair-
A manifestation of his sacrifice.

I stand
In reverence of my hero,
His bronze medal,
His pair of purple hearts.
Our country's waving emblem.
I am free because he was brave.

62. EMPTY CHAIR
Lauren Lyon, 2021

The boy sat in his chair with a fishing pole in hand
He gazed out at the lake
The bobber floating still
But the chair to his right was empty

The sun shined high at noon
Making the water glimmer and shine
The boy squinted and saw his bobber start to go under
But the chair to his right was empty

The line started to pull sending the boy into excitement
He started to reel in the fish, quickening with each second
He finally got the fish on the bank
and took it off the hook with a grin, he turned around to show his prize
But the chair to his right was empty

63. THE LAMPPOST

Lynnea Crock, 2021

A lamppost stands tall obeying,
its dignified duty to those who are lost in the dark,
Waiting to turn on at night,
And turn off at dawn.
Still, in daylight when it has no job, it sees.
It sees the people of the world.

The lamppost watches loved ones vanish,
Some temporarily and some forever.
It sees the kids scream for their parents,
As they hike up the bus stairs to the battlefield.
Kids of all ages,
Some too young to understand
and others who know the routine too well.
Some leave with suitcases and others leave with memories.

The lamppost watches people cross the bustling street,
Where cars don't even slow down.
The kids prance across it, holding the hands of their parents,
The teens don't look up from their phones,
And the elders wobble to the other side with much trouble
because no one bothers to help.
Instead the cars that await the white line honk at their pesky presence.
The elders feel bad for taking so long
and the citizens in the cars tap their feet,
But still they offer no hand in help.

Continued

The lamppost watches the strained face of a single mother place flowers
in the small grass yard where a cross was placed next to it.
The same crosswalk that hundreds pass over per day
killed the one love she had left,
For not seven years before, the lamppost saw the same woman with a
round tummy fighting with a man.
The man was holding a duffel bag and spitting words of hate,
Wanting nothing to do with her or her filthy child.
Her heart was shattered because of one person.
One person who was a little too distracted by the nude photo they had
received on their phone not moments before
they hit the innocent soul of her child.
The child who had a smile plastered on his face because he had lost his
first tooth and couldn't wait to show his mommy.

The lamppost watches the happy, newly married couple
kiss before parting in opposite directions for the day,
Until the woman started showing up with bruises covered in makeup.
It watches a teenage couple walk by holding hands
Fingers intertwined locking their love.
Then it sees the same girl with another boy the same day
and a different boy the next.

Continued

The lamppost watches the little girl who waits for the bus
in the morning by herself with an empty stomach.
It notices she never has a coat, a hat, or mittens in the winter,
And her shoes are worn with holes.
It watches her get off the bus with blood shot swollen eyes
from being made fun of,
Humiliated and pushed down.
Her parents never were there to pick her up.

She never forgot they loved her even if they did.
It saw the little girl grow into a beautiful young lady,
And then suddenly the girl stopped showing up for the bus.
Empty pill bottles, razor blades, and a tear-stained note.
When everyone found out what had happened,
their reactions bewildered the post.
Her parents frowned,
Her bullies laughed,
Her teachers sighed,
The lamppost cried,
And the world went on.

The lamppost sees heartbreak and tears.
It sees death and sadness.
It sees carelessness.
It watches a town who is filled with greed and selfishness.
But the thing it doesn't see enough of is a love for one another.
I've viewed this life through the eyes of the lamppost for years,
Sitting on a bench placed beside it and the cross of the child.
And still I wonder...if the lamppost had a heartbeat,
would it care anymore than anyone else?

64. CANNONBALL
Ella Dean, 2022

ONE. TWO. THREE. I am rolling down at what seems to be top speeds on a dusty mattress in the tightest ball my small frame can muster. I am down the mattress, and my forehead connects with the corner of the wall before I can say "CANNONBALL!" My mother came running up the steps at the sound, but I insisted I felt fine. I looked down for a moment and saw the most blood five-year-old me had seen up until that point. All because my best friend, Sadiya, and I wanted to roll down a slide. Sadiya and I have been inseparable ever since.

In 2009, when my father was deployed and my family moved back to Germany for the second time, I met some silly, dark-haired girl just three months younger than I. There was an instant connection, and our poor parents had to live with our near-constant shenanigans. From losing Sadiya's only pet—her gray hamster named Grace—to at least four live frogs hidden around my house, those three years we never left each other's side.

Every time I look in the mirror and see the scar on my forehead from that fateful tumble down that mattress smelling of disinfecting spray, I smile and remember how that was only the second time Sadiya and I had met and how it bonded and scarred us for life.

65. BEAUTIFUL SOLITUDE
Scott Moore, 2022

THE QUIETEST, most inconspicuous moments can be some of the most valuable. When the world slows down, one's mind can really expand. In these times I have discovered a little more about myself and the universe. One such time occurred in the summer before my junior year of high school, during the height of the COVID-19 pandemic. As the world had largely shut down, I had a lot of free time. Everyone was plunged into solitude, and many found it uncomfortable. However, silence can be comforting. The time spent alone with one's thoughts can reveal much about who he/she is.

Do other people experience such sensations the same as I do? If so, are we more alone or less alone? If everyone experienced the exact same sensations, then we would surely only see issues from one ignorant view. It is man's differences from his peers that allow the group to work toward finding meaning in the world. If we were all the same, we would all be hopelessly alone together. I decided to wish that nobody would be like I was, so that, though I would feel alone, other views might compliment my own to form a more sophisticated answer.

66. A TURTLE WITHOUT ITS SHELL
Daniel Swartz, 2023

Slow and passive, a turtle's nothing but docile.
With its mighty shell, who would dare attack?
It crawls and strides in confidence, it's anything but hostile.
"Impenetrable defense," is written on the shell, like a proud plaque.
A turtle doesn't have many things going on in its life.
The turtle only has one thing to be truly proud,
Its mighty shell for when it gets into strife.
Protecting is what the shell vowed.
But useless is a fox without its speed.
Useless is a fish without its gills.
Useless is a plant that produces no seed.
Useless is a hedgehog that has no quills.
It's a fact that everyone knows well,
That a turtle is useless without its shell.

67. CEMETERY
Selah Murphy, 2023

SHE FELT LIGHT as the gravediggers dropped the box slowly into the ground. Her mind too detached to grasp much of her surroundings, her focus was barely even tethered to the coffin. The hole seemed to reluctantly swallow the shoddy, crooked casket. A dull thud broke the silence, and the ropes went down after it.

The few others who came to mourn began to file away, sniffling lines of sentiment to her. She managed to nod her goodbyes, but never shifted her gaze from the gaping hole.

The hole the gravediggers were now unceremoniously refilling with dirt. They nudged each other, mumbling hushed discussions between them.

She knew there was no way their conversation had anything to do with her, or the life they had just signified the end of, but it raked on her eardrums. Their voices were condescending. The subtle, easy cadence of their commentary pooled jealousy in her skull. As quiet as it was, it overshadowed any words of sympathy directed toward her.

Their passing looks of familiarity as they went about their work made her heart ache. Her eyes darted between them, attempting to imagine making such comfortable expressions to another person again.

She couldn't seem to move, she felt that hands began to pull her shoulders down. Tears slid down her face as she leaned farther forward. Every step towards the present she had stayed at his side, had created a careful web of a life around his needs. It stung to see every other person had simply left.

Home was a chair beside his bed, her work, making him smile. Her life was him. And he took her life with him when he died. When *she* died.

The gravediggers were quick to pull her from the edge, attempting to stop her from hurting herself.

The edges of her vision began to go dark, a wonderful shadow that matched her own feelings. It was comforting. Sharp pains wracked her chest, but she was done, she wanted to give in to the simplicity in darkness.

Suddenly they began to shake her, to yell for a response. She closed her eyes and waited to see him again.

68. LET'S NOT GET POLITICAL
Lee Wilkins, 2023

How am I…
Supposed…
to exist?
How am I supposed to exist when I am watching the world fall?
Crumpling with the lies tumbling around me.

I hear their voices,
Their screams of fear and rage.
And I am to ignore them,
And exist.

How am I supposed to exist,
In a world where I don't have the chance to make my own choices.
In a world where people tell me to "not get political"
Human rights are not political.

And yet I still have to get out of my bed.
And go to a job that doesn't pay enough to afford anything.
And go to my last year of high school.
I don't even want to walk those halls.
To be faced with people who support the politicians
that take away my rights.

Continued

But even more, I don't want to face the people like me.
The people that are stuck in the same cycle of
"we can't do anything about it"
I can't face the silence of conversations
when a "political" topic comes up.

How am I supposed to exist?
In a world where I am being silenced.
I am a bullet in a gun that has more rights than I.
I am this bullet fired into the hearts of those who don't want to die.
I am this bullet used by people saying they are trying to help the new
generations.

It is those people that are using us as a weapon.
Claiming that it is what their all-powerful wishes.
When their all-powerful has no power over the majority.

I ask again, how am I supposed to exist.
In this silence,
In this world being ripped apart,
In this damage that others have caused.
I just want to exist in times where I have a rough idea of what lies ahead
of me.
Where I am not planning for a future that I might not even be a part of.

But "let's not get political"
It makes people uncomfortable
God forbid that you are uncomfortable
When my future is dying,
And pulling me down with it.

69. CHAOS IN THE ER

Marina Nickolozakes, 2023

IT WAS A PEACEFUL Sunday morning, I was sitting behind the desk, shivering as always, and had nothing to do. I saw the emergency room at its cleanest and there was no nose-scrunching smell yet. Out of boredom, I grabbed a cart and went around to each of the hospital rooms to restock the linens. The ER has to be the most confusing place to navigate. I make one turn and then I am lost because everything looks the same. I continued to push around my cart full of linens, trying to waste more time. Little did I know of the head-scratching scene, bizarre encounter, and crazy task that I was about to take part in.

As I was patiently waiting for a job to come up behind the nurse's desk, all of a sudden, the public safety officers came running through the doors yelling, "she is shaking!" The nurses immediately jumped up from the desk and scrambled to put on their gloves. They began running for the doors, and I sat there because that was all my volunteer position had to offer at that moment. As I was alarmed by the situation at hand, a few minutes later I saw the public safety officers carrying in this scrawny little woman who could not sit still and the nurses just shaking their heads. The nurses told me that they thought she had overdosed but the problem was the officers tried putting her in handcuffs, but she was so tiny she just slipped right on out of them and tried running away.

Continuing with my duties of the day, I sat and watched this little boy come in while being manhandled by his mother. I looked over at the public safety police officers and they let out a chuckle because they just knew this story was going to be a good one. The mother was frantic and claimed that her son had swallowed around 27 of her pills as well as some loose change that he had found on the floor. We looked at the kid and he looked at us with his disobedient smile. Mind you this kid had to have been around 6 years old, so we already knew this kid was a little rascal. As this was happening, I noticed the kid was sweeping the floor with this dirty Christmas doll that looked like it had been dragged through wet puddles and garbage. It is currently the middle of July, so the doll is out of place for other reasons than being dirty. We printed off a medical band and so I started to bend down to this kid's height, and as I was reaching to put his medical band on him, I felt his wet doll flop on top of my head. My initial thought was I am going to get lice. I could not believe it. This kid dared to swing this rag doll at my head while I was trying to help him. I just looked at the kid and he smiled back at me with this look of mischief. He knew exactly what he had done. I could see the nurses behind me trying to hold in their laughter because they could feel my pain. Trying to remain professional after I had just been slimed by this kid, I casually stepped away without showing my face of disgust and moved my attention onto the next patient.

Following the wet doll dropping, an ambulance rolled up delivering a man in a wheelchair. The emergency department was pretty busy at this point in the day, so the nurses asked me to help wheel this man inside. I jumped up and began rolling him and then all of a sudden, I felt him cough on me. It was the fact that this man made no effort to cover his mouth. I tried so hard to keep it together, putting aside the fact of how disgusting that was, and right when I thought things could not get any worse, the crew that had brought him said he had covid. I was thinking to myself, great, I just got right up on this guy, and I am only wearing a cheap disposable mask. The nurses handed me a medical band, making me take another step closer to this man, and as I asked him for his wrist he turned and coughed on me again! The cough hit me like a gust of wind, and I could just tell the germs coated me this time. Then the nurse asked me, oh so generously, if I would escort this kind man to the isolation room. At this point, I was thinking to myself how ridiculous this was, but that's not all. The final cherry on top happened right after I overheard the nurse make a Vocera call to the doctors, announcing that I was bringing the patient back to the isolation room and for them to get all suited up and put their hazmat suits on.

My days usually consist of this kind of craziness. The emergency department pulls all sorts of people: loud ones, self-pity ones, ones who think they are sick, and maybe ones who use the ER as a place to catch a break from the police. Whatever it may be, it sure keeps me entertained. Listening to the nurses judge the scoundrels that walk in and with all of this constant activity, there is never a dull moment. Without a head-scratching scene, bizarre encounter, and crazy task, it would not be a volunteer experience.

LIST OF WINNERS BY YEAR

Due to the constraints of modern publishing, we were unable to include every piece of writing from every winner over the years in this collection. We're publishing the names of each winner here to further acknowledge their achievement in winning the Susan Award with their writing.

2019 Adams, Avery	2011 Evans, Meredith	2023 Nickolozakes, Marina
2008 Adams, Chelsea	2004 Evans, Robert	2007 Parker, Abe
2004 Allen, Emmy	2018 Frame, Katie	2013 Parker, Grace
2004 Ankrum, Trisha	2011 Frank, Jazmin	2019 Perry, Austin
2008 Baptista, Shecky	2009 Gosnell, Lydia	2020 Pitcock, Adelaide
2016 Barry, Madeline	2006 Gress, Jessica	2021 Pollock, Samual
2020 Beane, Cambria	2006 Guilliams, Carrie	2003 Ray, Rita
2005 Beauchamp, Jesse	2013 Hamilton, Harley	2017 Reed, Miranda
2019 Bell, Chad	2004 Heskett, Emily	2005 Reiss, Brianne
2012 Bell, Megan	2015 Holbert, Olivia	2023 Roberts, Donathan
2016 Bird, Jacob	2014 Holdren, Sarah	2020 Salsbury, Alexis
2013 Bliss, Leandra	2010 Izer, Heather	2005 Semdley, Tegan
2007 Brothers, Abbigail	2021 Jackson, Murphy	2018 Shawger, Alyssa
2010 Bugglin, Taylor	2003 Johnson, Chris	2008 Shipitalo, Ellen
2019 Chambers, Sierra	2011 Kilpatrick, Mackrea	2017 Smith, Brittany
2016 Chittum, Kathryn	2020 Knicely, Megan	2010 Smith, Kaitlyn
2012 Coen, Anne	2012 Laube, Aaron	2007 Smith, Megan
2011 Collins, Karlie	2015 Leasure, Nicolette	2018 Stoepfel, Hannah
2013 Corns, Cameron	2015 Lekan, William	2023 Swartz, Daniel
2017 Cowden, Alayna	2010 Lowe, Rachel	2019 Timm, Ethan
2021 Crock, Lynnea	2021 Lyon, Lauren	2017 Van Horn, Bennett
2006 Culp, Mason	2008 Marsh, Cassandra	2013 Van Horn, Megan
2005 Darr, Derrick	2007 Martin, Erica	2018 Vejsicky, Sarah
2022 Dean, Ella	2003 McGuire, Kate	2011 Virostko, Katerina
2018 Dietz, Emily	2006 Mercer, Amber	2005 Wachtel, Douglas
2016 Dougherty, Kyle	2008 Mitchell, Tiffany	2016 Warschauer, Abigail
2014 Downing, Becky	2020 Moore, Ava	2021 Wehr, Nathan
2007 Dubosh, Nicole	2022 Moore, Scott T.	2009 Wheeler, Chelsea
2004 Eno, Josh	2023 Murphy, Selah	2023 Wilkins, Kaylee "Lee"
2006 Evans, Haley	2017 Myers, Madeline	2009 Wisenbarger, Angelica

TEACHERS OF RECIPIENTS

Allen, Tracy
River View High School

Collins, Jill
Ridgewood High School

Corbett, Nancy
Philo High School

Cox, Judy
River View High School

Day, Katie
John Glenn High School

DeVoll, Kimberley
Tri-Valley High School

DeVolld, Mary Ann
John Glenn High School

Edwards, Tiffany
Philo High School

Frank, Frederick
John Glenn High School

Graham, Heather
John Glenn High School

Morrison, Pamela
River View High School

Polous, Theresa
John Glenn High School

Prince, Mark
Tri-Valley High School

Rolling, Leah
John Glenn High School

Rotella, Raymond
Tri-Valley High School

Rucker, Cynthia
Maysville High School

Salsbury, Nancy
Philo High School

Schubert, Blythe
Morgan High School

Shawger, Jane
West Muskingum High School

Simko, Kathryn
Tri-Valley High School

Smoulder, Angela
Ridgewood High School

Smoulder, Jesse
River View High School

Snively, Susan
John Glenn High School

Stoepfel, Toni
Maysville High School

Wayne, Myra
Maysville High School

Weiser, Elizabeth
Tri-Valley High School

ACKNOWLEDGMENTS

JUDGES: Deep appreciation is extended to several dedicated former high school English teachers who for varying time periods across the twenty years, accepted the challenge of reading and assessing the extraordinary submissions of some 970 high school seniors.

> Mary Ann DeVolld
> Lynn Echard
> Cora Garrison
> Dottie Geyer
> Barb Hansen
> Gary Lucas
> Raymond Rotella

EDITORS: Gratitude is extended to Muskingum University's Education Studies Department for providing majors in its high school English Language Arts program to serve as editors, assessors, and typists for the preparation of the anthology.

> Olivia Angles
> Taylor Evans
> Emily Mullikin
> Bailee Shafer

THANKS TO: The Muskingum Valley Educational Service Center for communicating the contest details, handling the student submissions, and annually recognizing all student winners.

Muskingum County Community Foundation for serving as the fiscal agent for the Susan Award Fund.

East Muskingum Schools Student Endowment Fund for initiating the student recognition fund.

Wanda Read—East Muskingum Administrative Assistant for 20 years of organizing and filing over 970 student submissions.

Natasha Biggins, JGHS student, who assisted with editing, typing, and organizing the anthology.

Special thanks and acknowledgement to Dr. Barbara Hansen, whose tireless work with students made this publication possible. She has been continuously unwavering with support since the inception of the award over twenty ago, with her selfless devotion and professional judgements.